HYDRANGEA PUBLISHING

HYDRANGEA PUBLISHING
2295 NW Corporate Boulevard, Suite 117,
Boca Raton, Florida 33431

ISBNs:
eBook   979-8-9899320-0-9
Paperback   979-8-9899320-1-6
Hardcover   979-8-9899320-2-3
LCCN   2024903857

First Edition
Book Production and Publishing by *Brands Through Books*
brandsthroughbooks.com

www.HydrangeaPublishing.com

L.A. PERKINS

TOP-RATED INTELLECTUAL PROPERTY ATTORNEY

WHY BRAND PROTECTION MATTERS

How to Avoid Costly Mistakes and
Increase the Value of Your Business

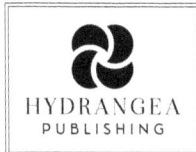

HYDRANGEA
PUBLISHING

"*Why Brand Protection Matters* makes it easy for nonlawyers to understand exactly how they should be protecting their brand assets and the importance of doing so. If you value your business, this book is a must-read."

—JEANNETTE KNUDSEN, Chief Legal Officer,
The J.M. Smucker Co.

"*Why Brand Protection Matters* emphasizes that the devil is in the details in the very best of ways. Perkins' comprehensive guide underscores the essentiality of the brand protection process and the complexity of the laws surrounding it while also highlighting the benefits of diligent brand protection. This book is not just a publication; it's a roadmap businesses can use to navigate the challenging yet rewarding journey of protecting their brand."

—RICHARD "RICHIE" SISKIND, Founder and Chairman of
R Siskind & Co and Skechers Board Member

"Protecting a company's intellectual property should be priority number one because if you don't, you will lose your biggest strategic advantage. As a mentor and angel investor for startups, I always stress the critical importance of protecting intellectual property, and I urge business owners to read *Why Brand Protection Matters* so they can gain the knowledge and insight they need to make informed decisions about the best path for them."

—RICHARD HERBERT, former President and
Chief Operating Officer, Pantone Inc.

"*Why Brand Protection Matters* provides an easy to read and understandable description of intellectual property law and the process of brand protection (patents, trademarks, copyrights, trade secrets). It lays out why it is important to protect a business's brand assets and how to avoid costly and protracted litigation. An excellent primer, with helpful and valuable information."

—MANUEL MENENDEZ JR., mediator and retired
Chief Judge, 13th Judicial Circuit of Florida

"*Why Brand Protection Matters* is a great read! L.A. Perkins is a real thought leader and writes about important lessons that all business owners should know about protecting their brand. I highly recommend this book."

—GARY S. LESSER, Managing Partner of Lesser, Lesser, Landy &
Smith, PLLC and former President of The Florida Bar

IN MEMORY OF MY LOVING AND
COURAGEOUS PARENTS
ARNOLD AND MARSHA PERKINS

Contents

A NOTE TO THE READER

THIS BOOK IS INTENDED TO PROVIDE GENERAL INFORMATION and insights about the importance of brand protection and information relating thereto. While the author, L.A. Perkins, is a licensed attorney in the State of Florida, the information in this book should not be considered legal advice. The content contained in this book is for educational and informational purposes only. This book does not create an attorney-client relationship between L.A. Perkins and the reader.

Readers are strongly encouraged to consult with a qualified legal professional regarding their specific situation or legal issue. Laws and regulations vary and are subject to change, and the application of legal principles can vary based on individual facts and circumstances. The content of this book may not reflect the most current legal developments or all aspects of a particular legal issue.

While efforts were made to ensure the accuracy and completeness of the information provided, no warranty or representation, express or implied, is made as to the accuracy or completeness of the content.

By reading this book, you acknowledge and agree to the terms of this disclaimer.

Who This Book Is for And How It Will Help

WHEN IT COMES TO BRAND PROTECTION, THE DEVIL IS IN THE details. It does not pay to be penny-wise and pound-foolish by either doing it yourself or hiring an inexperienced brand protection, intellectual property, or trademark attorney (these terms are used interchangeably throughout the book). Doing so, from my experience, often costs more money in the long run. In fact, the involvement of experienced legal representation in the trademark application process correlates with higher success rates of businesses being protected.[1]

Whether you are at the beginning stages of starting a business or already have a business and want to make sure that it is protected, this book is written for you. Knowledge is power. Congratulations on taking action to ensure your brand is protected. I am delighted that you chose to read this book, and I am committed to making it worth your time.

I will share valuable information and tips based on my more than 27 years of experience as an entrepreneur and attorney who helps clients protect their brand assets and represents clients in court—tips that most entrepreneurs, business owners, and non-IP attorneys, in my experience, do not know.

As a brand protection attorney, I have worked with clients to brainstorm possible trademarks and guided clients in selecting protectable brands. It is my custom to roll up my sleeves and learn about my clients' businesses so that I can help them identify what IP assets they have that need protecting and to then come up with a strategic plan to do so and implement the plan. I have prepared and filed trademark and copyright applications. I have helped clients monitor their trademarks for infringing use and have sent out and responded to numerous cease and desist letters (also referred to as demand letters) on behalf of my clients. I have filed lawsuits, defended clients across the country, and helped clients amicably resolve intellectual property disputes without needing to engage in litigation that would be costly for all parties involved.

As an entrepreneur, I know what it is like to start a business with limited resources, where you are laser-focused on getting up and running so you can start earning money and you tell yourself everything will fall into place down the road. I also know what it is like to move forward full steam ahead and then hit a brick wall. While in college, I started two businesses. I took no action to protect the businesses' intellectual property or to make sure I was not infringing upon other companies' intellectual property rights. Frankly, I did not know any better at the time. I share more of those experiences, as well as what I have since learned, throughout this book. Today, I have my own law firm, and since I now know better, I can do better. I have taken action to protect, and have protected, my firm's intellectual property assets, and I will continue to do so. I was inspired to write this book because I believe all business owners should be aware of the benefits of smart brand protection practices and be armed with the knowledge of the information contained in this book.

THE AMERICAN DREAM

The American dream of having my own business became the guiding force for my life when, on July 4, 1986, I attended the largest naturalization ceremony in the history of the United States.[2] I was 17 years old, a junior in high school. My mother and brother were beside me. The stadium was full. We were among 14,000 immigrants in the Miami Orange Bowl, all proudly taking an oath to become citizens of the United States. The excitement in the air was palpable. The energy was festive and hopeful. It was a huge celebration with fireworks and congratulatory, inspiring remarks by then-President Ronald Reagan and other officials.

As I took the oath to become a citizen of this great country, I was overcome with emotions. With tears rolling down my face, I reflected on the sacrifices my parents made so that my brother and I could have a better life. At that moment, I made the decision and became determined to make the most of my life in honor of my parents, which included giving back and making a difference for others. I felt (and still feel) truly blessed to have the opportunity to be a citizen of the United States—the land of opportunity, as my parents often referred to the U.S. The faces of the many kind and generous people who helped me and my family along the way flashed through my thoughts. There were many people who helped us. I consider them angels in my life, and I am forever grateful for them.

WITNESSING THE TRIALS AND TRIBULATIONS OF A BUSINESS OWNER

We immigrated from Johannesburg, South Africa, in 1977 as a family—my father, mother, brother, and me. My father started an Italian tile and carpeting business in Miami, Florida, named

Medici (pronounced Medeechi). It was back then that I first noticed what it meant to begin and work in a business built from the ground up. I witnessed my father's trials and tribulations as a business owner and asked lots of questions—I was interested in his business and how it worked from an early age. I enjoyed going to work with him on the weekends, observing him, and listening to his conversations.

Unfortunately, my father was not with us as we took our oath of citizenship. My parents divorced when I was 12. Sadly, soon after, my father was diagnosed with bone cancer and returned to South Africa. He passed away when I was 19 years old—the year after I graduated from high school. Thankfully, my father lived long enough to experience great joy and satisfaction when my mother, brother, and I became citizens of the United States.

I am immensely grateful for all I learned about business from my father and for how he inspired me to explore being a business owner. Now, my father's entrepreneurial spirit and legacy live on through me. I also see signs of his legacy continuing through my son, who is working toward starting his own business.

LAYING THE FOUNDATION FOR BEING A BUSINESS OWNER

I dreamed of having a business of my own one day. While attending Miami Sunset Senior High School, I took a class called Street Law and loved learning about the law. I signed up to participate in our high school mock trial team. Our team won the mock trial competition, and we represented the State of Florida in Washington, DC, where we competed nationally. I knew at that point that I wanted to be an attorney. In addition to the law being an honorable profession that would provide me with the opportunity to make a difference, I also wanted a career where I would be able to financially take care of myself and my family. I saw my mother struggle financially as a single parent and wanted to make sure I did not perpetuate that struggle for myself.

While my plan was to go to law school, I wanted my undergraduate degree to be in business. I thought that would make me more well-rounded in the practice of law and provide me with an education that would help me in my entrepreneurial endeavors. Marketing always fascinated me. As a child, I loved inspecting packaging and observing how companies promoted themselves. Little did I know back then that my interest in marketing would serve me well as an intellectual property attorney. I earned my associate of arts degree from Miami Dade College on a full Junior Achievement of Greater Miami scholarship following teaching the Junior Achievement Business Basics course to elementary school children while I was in high school. Afterward, I obtained my bachelor of business administration degree in international finance and marketing from the University of Miami, with honors. I was blessed with a partial scholarship, financial aid, and student loans to be able to attend the University of Miami.

OATH OF ADMISSION

My dream of becoming an attorney was realized in 1996 after I graduated from Stetson University College of Law (Florida's oldest law school) that same year. I remember taking the Oath of Admission to become an attorney in the State of Florida like it was yesterday. With thoughts flashing back to the day I took my oath of citizenship of the United States and all I had gone through to get to that point in my life, I beamed with pride and was hopeful about my future.

Below is a photo of now-retired Judge Manuel Menendez Jr. of the 13th Judicial Circuit of Florida (whom I had the honor of interning for while in law school) in his chambers, swearing me in as an attorney of The Florida Bar on December 2, 1996.

LEGAL PRACTICE AND BREAKING INTO PRACTICING INTELLECTUAL PROPERTY LAW

Since then, I have had the good fortune to serve as counsel to a wide array of clients—from individuals to Fortune 100 companies in various industries. When I first became an attorney, I focused my practice on employment law. While I enjoyed employment law, I began seeking opportunities to practice intellectual property law in my second year of practice. My break came in about my sixth year of practice when a pharmaceutical client of the law firm I had recently joined was served with a lawsuit and an order to appear before a federal judge in Colorado for a temporary injunction hearing in two days' time, which was the day before Christmas. The partner handling the matter needed help preparing for the hearing. I offered to assist, making sure he understood that while I was confident with my research and writing skills, I would need guidance because the legal issues were, at that time, new to me. We flew to Colorado and worked through the night writing a brief in opposition to the injunction request and preparing for the hearing. The lawyers on the other side were from a large, highly regarded national law firm. We won the hearing and were notified that the business that had sought the injunction ended up dropping their case by the time we arrived at the airport for our return flight home. That was a thrilling day and the start of me handling intellectual property law matters.

WHAT IS LIKELY ON YOUR MIND

If you are reading this book, I suspect you have a big vision for your business. You are likely determined to do whatever is necessary to maximize the success of your business. I also suspect you are innovative and committed to making a difference for your customers with the goods or services you sell. I further suspect you want your business to thrive so you can provide for your family and ensure your family members have bright futures and financial security. I respect that and can relate to you. Perhaps you dream of selling your business down the road so you can comfortably retire and leave a legacy for your family. You likely want to make sure you "dot your i's and cross your t's" so your business is well-positioned for growth and success.

If you are reading this book, you likely know that having a unique and widely recognizable company name, logo, and slogan that belongs only to your company is important for the success of your business. However, you may be uncertain about what brand protection is and whether it is necessary for YOUR business. You may be wondering whether brand protection is something you can put off until sometime down the road when your business is more successful. You may also be wondering whether you can do what is required to protect your brand yourself or whether it is necessary to hire an attorney to help you. You may also be uncertain about the process and who the right person is to help you and guide you in protecting your brand. You may be wondering when the right time is to take action to protect your brand. You may find yourself distracted with thoughts and concerns about whether you have protected your brand correctly or whether there is something you need to do that you have not done. You may also be wondering whether the cost associated with working with an attorney is worth it. And, if you are like most of my clients, you may not know what needs to be protected in your business.

These thoughts—that little voice in the back of your head—are likely distracting you from your business and all that matters to you. The uncertainty and, perhaps, fear of the unknown are likely creating unnecessary stress and anxiety for you, which are robbing you of clarity and peak performance. I can relate. There have been times in my life when I have been uncertain about what action to take: times when I struggled with what would be the right thing to do, what would be the right way to do it, and whether I could do it myself; times where I felt frustrated and anxious. These feelings persisted for me until I engaged a professional with the relevant expertise to help me.

MY COMMITMENT TO YOU

When you have finished reading this book, you will be empowered to protect your company's brand assets. Not only will this book provide you with clarity and knowledge about the importance of brand protection and the process, you will also learn the fundamentals of creating and maintaining a legally protectable brand. You will be empowered to limit your risk of being blindsided and potentially derailed by legal issues that could cost you your business and all of your hard-earned money. You will also be empowered to build your business on a solid foundation so that it is set up for success.

Many legal issues that arise in businesses, including trademark infringement, can be avoided. In this book, I will explain how you can minimize your risk of receiving a threatening letter from another company (often a competitor with deep pockets)—referred to as a cease and desist letter or demand letter—accusing you and your company of trademark infringement, threatening to file a lawsuit, claiming you owe hundreds of thousands of dollars or more, and demanding that you immediately cease using your company's name. You will also learn valuable information that will enable you to have intelligent and streamlined conversations with an attorney, resulting in saving you time and money.

If you are in the process of setting up a business or developing a new product or service, you will learn how to select a name, logo, or slogan that is legally protectable. You will also learn how to determine if a potential name, logo, or slogan infringes on another company's intellectual property rights.

If you are already in business and have been operating under a brand name, you will learn how to determine whether there is a company with a similar name, logo, or slogan and, if that is the case, what actions to take, which will depend on the context. For example, important details to consider include whether the other company's use predates or postdates your company's first use of the name, logo, or slogan and whether the other company has already obtained a trademark registration. If the other company's use predates your date of first use, the other company will be deemed to have senior rights, and you will not have leverage to stop them from continuing to use the mark. If the other company obtained a trademark registration for the same or similar mark for the same, similar, or related goods or services, you will likely not be successful in obtaining exclusive trademark rights.

You will also learn how to determine whether the name, logo, or slogan you are using can be legally protected so that you may obtain exclusive rights to use those brand assets in the United States. If you have already engaged in some brand protection on your own, a trademark attorney will be able to review what you have done to ensure whether it was done correctly or if tweaks and additional action are necessary.

Let's dive in!

CHAPTER 1

Do Not Delay—Benefits of Brand Protection

THIS BOOK FOCUSES ON UNITED STATES TRADEMARK PROTECTION because it is the most important type of intellectual property (IP) when securing national rights to your company's brand name, logo, and slogan. However, it will also include some important information to know about other areas of intellectual property (that is, copyright, patent, and trade secret protection). I want you to be able to avoid common, costly mistakes.

I suspect you have a very busy life where you juggle many things; that is the life of an entrepreneur and business owner, and I can relate. I want to acknowledge you for taking (or should I say making) the time to read this book so you can learn very important information and be able to protect your business. I am excited about the difference the information contained in this book can make in your business and your life.

ACT SOONER VERSUS LATER

So, do you want to know when the right time is to take action to protect the brand name, logo, or slogan under which you are selling your goods or services? Here is the short answer: the sooner the better. Being the first to take action to obtain a federal trademark registration will prevent another company from obtaining one for the same or similar mark for the same or similar goods or services. You see, when you file a federal trademark application, you are putting a proverbial stake in the ground, claiming exclusive ownership in the United States of the name, logo, or slogan (often referred to as your "mark") related to the goods or services your business is selling or intends to sell. You want to do this before any other individual or company beats you to it by filing a trademark application before you do. In fact, it may be prudent to file more than one trademark application if your company has created and is using more than one brand name, logo, or slogan.

Have you heard the expression, "If you snooze, you lose"? Well, when it comes to trademarks, that old expression is certainly true. Below is an example where delaying can negatively impact your ability to secure federal trademark protection.

TEN-YEAR CO. AND PRUDENT CO. EXAMPLE— WHAT CAN HAPPEN IF ACTION IS DELAYED

Let's say a business that has been operating for more than ten years in three different states in the United States decides it is time to seek counsel to protect its brand—the company name under which its services are being sold. I will refer to this company as Ten-Year Co.

Ten-Year Co. wants to determine whether it could be successful in filing a trademark application to protect its company brand. A comprehensive trademark search reveals that another company located in a different state filed a trademark application with the United States Patent and Trademark Office (USPTO) six months earlier stating its "intent to use" the same brand name as Ten-Year Co.—I will refer to that proactive company as Prudent Co. Not

WHY BRAND PROTECTION MATTERS

only did Prudent Co. claim the same name as Ten-Year Co., it also intends to sell the same type of goods. Even though Ten-Year Co. was in business first and already using the trademark, its company brand, Prudent Co. will still be able to proceed with obtaining a federal trademark registration for the same name because no other federal trademark registration for the same mark exists.

You see, a trademark application may be filed as an intent-to-use application, which essentially states that an entity is not currently using the trademark but plans to do so within the next few years, thereby putting its proverbial stake in the ground and putting everyone on notice. Alternatively, a trademark application may be filed as an "in use" application. The saying "The early bird gets the worm" (meaning someone will have an advantage if they do something right away or before anyone else does it) certainly holds true when it comes to protecting your brand.

Now, Ten-Year Co. does have some options due to what are called "common law rights," having discovered that there is a pending trademark application for the brand name it has been using. Among other things, it can contest or oppose Prudent Co.'s trademark application, but it does not have as much leverage as it would have if it had a registered trademark. I discuss contesting or opposing trademark applications in chapter nine.

Ten-Year Co. could contest Prudent Co.'s trademark application, claiming a "likelihood of confusion" with its common law trademark. This analysis is factually specific, and no two likelihood of confusion claims are the same. Such a claim also comes at a substantial financial cost and with a lot of aggravation because it generally sidetracks the company engaging in the dispute from focusing on running its business. However, if Ten-Year Co. wants to stop Prudent Co. from using the company name in addition to blocking the federal trademark registration and Prudent Co. will not voluntarily agree, Ten-Year Co. will need to file a lawsuit seeking the entry of a court order precluding Prudent Co. from continuing to use the disputed company name.

If Prudent Co. obtains a trademark registration from the USPTO, Ten-Year Co. will be able to continue to use its brand name in the jurisdictions where it was used prior to the date Prudent Co. filed its federal trademark application, but it will not be able to use its brand name outside of those areas, thereby impacting Ten-Year Co.'s ability to expand its business using its brand name. If Ten-Year Co. expands into other areas after Prudent Co. obtains a registered trademark, Ten-Year Co. will expose its business to being sued for trademark infringement. The bottom line is that because Ten-Year Co. waited and did not seek counsel to protect its brand sooner, it will likely be precluded from having national rights to its brand name. However, if Ten-Year Co. does business outside of the United States, it could seek to protect its brand name in jurisdictions outside of the United States even though it does not have a registered United States trademark.

In my practice, I have seen numerous companies restricted from obtaining exclusive trademark rights to a brand name in the U.S. because another company acted before them in filing a trademark application with the USPTO (or began using the mark sooner).

Benefits of Federal Trademark Registration

There are numerous reasons why you should care about protecting your brand sooner instead of later. Protecting your company's brand is important whether you are an aspiring or longtime business owner, as can be gleaned from the Ten-Year Co./Prudent Co.

example shared above. To protect your company's brand, you need to identify what intellectual property assets you have and what actions need to be taken to properly protect those valuable assets.

Registration Provides Exclusive Rights of Use

By obtaining a United States trademark for your company's brands, you safeguard your company's intellectual property from competitors using the same mark you selected and position yourself to prevent copycats from profiting off selling similar goods or services using your company's brand identifiers nationally. By no means am I suggesting that protecting your brand identifiers (word mark, design mark or logo, or slogan) fully insulates you from these types of issues; however, having a registered United States trademark puts others on notice that you claim national and exclusive rights to use your company's particular brand identifier, thereby warding off others from using the same identifier to sell similar goods or services throughout the United States. In addition, a company with a properly registered United States trademark is in the best position to be able to protect its business from infringers.

Registration Provides Notice of Your Exclusive Use of the Trademark

In addition to having exclusive rights to use the mark associated with the goods or services you sell nationally, there are other benefits to having a trademark registered with the USPTO. When you have a registered trademark, your trademark is listed on the USPTO register of trademarks and can show up in searches, thereby deterring others from using the same mark. You also have the right to use the ® symbol following your mark to put everyone on notice that it is a registered trademark (versus using ™ follow-ing your mark, indicating you are using the mark as a trademark but that it is not registered). The ® acts as a deterrent to others wanting to use the same mark. Without the use of the registration symbol, other companies may not know of your rights.

Registration Provides Additional Remedies to Enforce Your Rights

With a registered trademark, you have the right to file a lawsuit in federal court and recover statutory damages. Statutory damages are a monetary award. The federal statute that governs trademark law in the United States is the Lanham Act. Under the Lanham Act, a judge in federal court has broad discretion to award $1,000–$200,000 in statutory damages for non-willful infringement and up to $2 million for willful infringement for each type of good or service infringed upon.[3] The threat of statutory damages can play an important role in resolving a dispute with an accused infring-er because it can make it easier for a trademark owner to obtain monetary damages.

Registration Provides Leverage When Sending a Cease and Desist Letter

When you have a registered trademark and send a cease and desist letter to a company that you believe is infringing upon your rights, having a registered trademark provides you with more leverage and the proverbial teeth needed in the negotiation process. As a business owner, you can send a cease and desist letter on your own. However, it bears mentioning here that you will likely be taken more seriously if you have a brand protection attorney prepare and send the cease and desist letter on your behalf. The attorney will be able to inform and guide you on your options and then properly state your position so that you do not end up inadvertently creating more issues for yourself by misstating your position.

Registration Provides Opportunities to Monetize Your Brand Through Licensing and Franchising

Licensing

Importantly, with a registered trademark, you are in a far better position to monetize your brand through licensing its use to another company. Licensing your brand can create additional income for your company. When you license a brand, you contractually allow another company to use your intellectual property in association with the goods or services it produces or sells. In addition to generating royalties, which are calculated based on a percentage of total sales or net profits, you also may be able to obtain an advance payment for the license, depending on the terms agreed to in the licensing agreement. However, there are requirements when licensing a brand that must be in place to maintain your trademark. An example of brand licensing is when the Walt Disney Company gave Timex the ability to produce watches featuring Mickey Mouse.[4]

Naked Licensing

Whenever I think of licensing, I always remember a case I worked on early in my career. The case involved two security companies with similar names. During that case, I learned about the concept of naked licensing. Sounds sexy, right? It is not. Being accused of naked licensing can be a nightmare for a trademark owner. Naked licensing is often a defense asserted by a company accused of using a trademark without permission to try to invalidate a mark.

A trademark owner can lose—yes, lose—their trademark rights by engaging in naked licensing, resulting in them not being able to prevent others from using their trademark. So, what is naked licensing? Naked licensing is when a trademark owner licenses the use of their trademark without sufficient quality controls in place over the licensee's use of the trademark. The concept is that, due to not having sufficient quality controls in place, the trademark no longer represents the quality initially associated with the goods or services being sold.

After a lengthy and expensive litigation battle, we were successful in establishing that the large security company that sued our client engaged in naked licensing, resulting in it losing its exclusive trademark rights. As a result, the large security company, which had obtained a U.S. federal trademark registration, was not able to stop our client, who did not have a registered trademark, from continuing to use their similar company name in the region in which they operated.

Franchising

A registered trademark is also important to have if you ever want to franchise your business. Licensing is similar to franchising, but it is not the same thing. Unlike licensing, where a company grants rights to use a registered trademark, a franchise is a more involved business relationship where a company allows another company to use its entire brand and operations. Examples of well-known franchises include McDonald's, 7-Eleven, Subway, Burger King, and Pizza Hut.

Registration Provides the Ability to Protect Your Brand with U.S. Customs and Border Protection

As part of a comprehensive plan to protect its brand, a company with a registered trademark or trademarks may register those marks with U.S. Customs and Border Protection (CBP) to receive border enforcement of its registered trademarks (and copyrights). A U.S. registered trademark is required to protect against the importation of goods in the United States bearing the same mark as your registered trademark. These unauthorized, inauthentic, infringing goods are commonly referred to as "counterfeit goods." The reason a company records its registered trademarks with CBP is to block counterfeit goods from entering the United States marketplace. Counterfeit products can irreparably harm your company's brand if a consumer has a negative experience with a counterfeit product thinking it is your company's product.

After a company records its trademarks with CBP, CBP will be on the lookout for attempts to import infringing goods. If such goods are found, it has the authority to detain, seize, forfeit, and destroy these items. The trademark owner is alerted of potential counterfeit products and is allowed to review the goods for authenticity. To help ensure CBP catches counterfeit products at the ports of entry, a trademark owner should be proactive and report suspicions concerning imported goods.

Registration Increases the Value of Your Business

Another very important benefit of a registered trademark is that it increases the value of your company because you have a market advantage—that is, the exclusive right to use the trademark. Legal protection of your company's trademarks (and other intellectual property) will increase the value of your company's intangible assets more so than if these assets remained unprotected. With a higher value, your company is in a stronger position to obtain financing when needed, and your company's market price will increase should you desire to sell down the road.

Today, IP assets comprise a very large part of the valuation of a company. The significance of IP assets with regard to valuation has increased over the years. According to a study conducted in 2020, intangible assets (the majority of which are intellectual property assets) are estimated to account for 90 percent of the total assets held by companies in the S&P 500.[5] As reflected in the chart below, this compares to 17 percent in 1975 and 68 percent in 1995. Clearly, IP assets are very significant.

COMPONENTS *of* S&P 500 MARKET VALUE

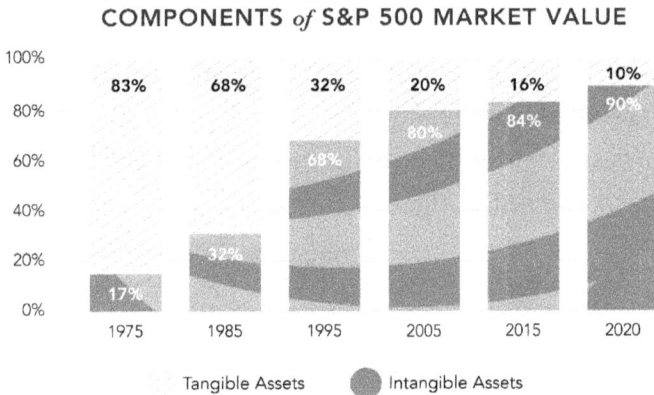

Ocean Tomo, a part of J.S. Held, Intangible Asset Market Value Study, 2020;
https://oceantomo.com/intangible-asset-market-value-study/

For example, one of my clients was able to substantially increase her negotiating position for the sale of her business because she had obtained a U.S. registered trademark. By being able to show the prospective buyer that she had taken all the necessary steps to protect and maintain her company's trademark rights, the offer price increased by 900 percent. My client was rewarded for her brand protection efforts and sold her company for more money than she ever imagined was possible.

There are many nuances to consider when protecting your brand. In my experience, many companies do not even realize that they are unprotected due to their misconceptions. In the following chapter, I will reveal common mistakes business owners make related to brand protection so that you are in the know and can avoid these pitfalls.

CHAPTER 2

Common Mistakes That Leave Your Brand Unprotected

OFTENTIMES, DURING AN INITIAL CONSULTATION WITH A POTEN-tial client who has run into a legal issue relating to their company name, the potential client professes they took all necessary steps to protect their company's brand. But as I ask questions and dig deeper, it turns out that they do not have the protection they thought they had. They are usually upset, frustrated, and disappointed with the news and sometimes even want to debate it with me, explaining that they followed the advice of another attorney or friend. I then put them at ease by explaining that the mistake they made is common and acknowledge them for being proactive by seeking professional counsel. These potential clients contact my firm because they discover that another company is using the same or a confusingly similar name as their business, and they want to stop that competing company from doing so.

In my experience, there are ten common mistakes business owners make when it comes to brand protection that cause them to think their brands are protected when they are not.

COMMON MISTAKE NUMBER ONE:
REGISTERING YOUR COMPANY NAME BY SETTING UP A CORPORATE ENTITY WITHOUT ALSO GETTING EXCLUSIVE USE TO THE COMPANY NAME

Registering your company's name or trade name (also referred to as a "doing business as" or "d/b/a" name) in a particular jurisdiction does not give you exclusive rights to use the name. For example, let's say you search the secretary of state records for the state in which you do business and find no other entity using the name you seek to register. You think this is great, and you believe you have the green light to register the company with the secretary of state. You then proceed with registering the company, believing you now own the name and have exclusive rights to it. However, trade name registration in a particular state only allows you to do business in that particular state under the registered name; it does not create exclusivity of the company name or a registered trademark with all the rights federal registration provides.

COMMON MISTAKE NUMBER TWO:
OBTAINING A DOMAIN NAME WITHOUT ALSO GETTING EXCLUSIVE RIGHTS TO USE THAT NAME

Let's say you own a domain name that is your company's brand name and believe you have exclusive rights to that company name. Unfortunately, domain name registration does not in and of itself provide your company with exclusive rights to use that brand name because it does not qualify as a "source identifier." In trademark law, a source identifier refers to something that distinguishes the origin of a particular product or service. Registration of a domain name with a domain name registrar does not create registered trademark rights. A domain name registration merely (although I do not mean to minimize it, as domain names are important) provides a web address for your company's website. Note that, even if you have a registered domain name, you may still be required to surrender the domain name later if it infringes on another company's trademark rights (see chapter three for a discussion on trademark infringement).

COMMON MISTAKE NUMBER THREE:
THINKING FIRST USE OF AN UNREGISTERED TRADEMARK IN A PARTICULAR JURISDICTION PREVENTS A COMPETITOR FROM OBTAINING NATIONAL TRADEMARK RIGHTS

Another common mistake is believing that because you started using your company's name first, another company cannot obtain a registered trademark with the USPTO for the same name. This is simply not true. Instead, if there are no conflicting registered trademarks, the USPTO will allow the applied-for trademark to be registered. Therefore, the burden is on the company that first used the mark to contest any trademark applications that are filed with the USPTO for the same or similar mark. For example, if you have a business in Miami, Florida, with a unique brand name and another company obtains a registered trademark for the same or similar brand name, if you used the name first, the company that has the registered trademark will not be able to stop you from using the brand name. However, if the company that obtained the registered trademark also operates in Miami, Florida, this may create confusion between the two companies (especially if it is a competing company), and you will need to take action to stop the competing company from using the brand name that you used first.

COMMON MISTAKE NUMBER FOUR:
ASSUMING THAT BECAUSE YOU ARE NOT AWARE OF ANOTHER COMPANY USING YOUR BRAND NAME, THE COAST IS CLEAR TO OBTAIN A TRADEMARK REGISTRATION WITH THE USPTO

Relying on your personal knowledge of the market to inform you of whether the brand name you are hoping to protect is not being used by any other company is a mistake. In other words, it is wrong to assume that if you do not know about a competing business with a similar name, you can secure a trademark without any issues. Rather, the truth is that an entity you are unaware of can file an objection to your trademark application, block you from obtaining the trademark registration with the USPTO, and even possibly prevent you from being able to continue to use the trademark you are seeking to protect.

COMMON MISTAKE NUMBER FIVE:
ATTEMPTING TO PERFORM A COMPREHENSIVE TRADEMARK SEARCH WITHOUT AN ATTORNEY

A common mistake is not conducting a thorough and comprehensive trademark search to make sure no other parties are using your mark before moving forward. Anyone can conduct a trademark search. However, most people cannot conduct the same type of comprehensive search that is done by experienced trademark attorneys. A comprehensive trademark search includes the review and analysis of various databases and sources including the USPTO, secretary of state records of all states in the U.S., social media platforms, et cetera. If you do not know whether your mark is the same or similar to marks in all of these databases, you could easily end up using a company name that infringes on another company's rights. This creates substantial risk. Therefore, comprehensive trademark searches should be performed by an attorney who can analyze the results and help determine the likelihood of being able to obtain a registered U.S. trademark and whether you may be at risk if you continue to use the mark in your business (see detailed discussion on searches in chapter seven).

COMMON MISTAKE NUMBER SIX:
NOT KNOWING WHAT INTELLECTUAL PROPERTY ASSETS YOU HAVE AND, THEREFORE, FAILING TO TAKE STEPS TO PROTECT THOSE ASSETS

Not being aware of what IP assets can be protected and, therefore, failing to put strategies and structures in place to protect those IP assets is a common mistake. Therefore, it is critical for companies to conduct a routine review of their IP assets to account for what they have and be informed on what can be done to protect those assets. I discuss the importance of IP audits more fully in chapter four.

COMMON MISTAKE NUMBER SEVEN:
FILING A TRADEMARK APPLICATION WITH INCORRECT DATES OF FIRST USE OR NOT KEEPING EVIDENCE OF THE DATES OF FIRST USE

Failing to keep accurate documentation of how, when, and where you first used your trademarks and not keeping track on an ongoing basis of how, when, and where you have continued to use your marks in business are common mistakes. Evidence of a company's date of first use of a mark can be a critical factor when securing and enforcing trademark rights. In chapter 11, I discuss that one of the reasons trademarks are canceled is that the information provided to the USPTO was not accurate.

An example of evidence of first use is a screenshot of your website on the date it went live with the URL and date showing the trademark in use in association with the goods or services in the trademark application. If your rights are ever challenged, you will need this information. For example, a company may seek to cancel your trademark rights if you fail to consistently use the trademark in commerce related to the goods or services associated with your registered trademark. Under the Lanham Act, a mark will be deemed abandoned if there is evidence that the mark is not being used and there is no proof of intent to resume use of the mark. Intent not to resume use may be inferred from the circumstances. Further, if there is no use of the mark in association with the sale of the goods or services identified in the trademark registration for three consecutive years, the USPTO will presume the mark has become abandoned and cancel the registration.

COMMON MISTAKE NUMBER EIGHT:
THINKING BRAND PROTECTION IS NOT A PRIORITY AND NOT BUDGETING FOR IT

Not having a budget for brand protection is a common mistake. When creating a budget to protect your company's IP assets, there are numerous factors to consider regarding the amount to budget, including the number of word marks, logos or design marks, and slogans your company intends to use or is currently using. Other factors to consider include the various geographic jurisdictions in which a company sells or intends to sell its goods or services.

COMMON MISTAKE NUMBER NINE:
THINKING A UNITED STATES TRADEMARK REGISTRATION PROVIDES PROTECTION OUTSIDE OF THE UNITED STATES

Not protecting your brand in jurisdictions where you sell or intend to sell your goods or services is a common mistake. A U.S. trademark registration does not provide exclusive rights to use your mark outside of the U.S. Therefore, if you are selling or intend to sell your goods or services in jurisdictions outside of the U.S., you should explore whether it makes business sense for you to protect your trademark in those other jurisdictions.

COMMON MISTAKE NUMBER TEN:
THINKING IT IS NOT NECESSARY TO USE A BRAND PROTECTION ATTORNEY

Trying to protect your brand assets on your own, using a nonlawyer service, or by retaining an inexperienced attorney is a common mistake. While business owners frequently attempt to do this thinking that it will save time and money, taking this approach commonly backfires. Also, taking the do-it-yourself approach increases the likelihood of making critical mistakes during the application process itself as well as when attempting to enforce or defend your IP rights.

Over the years, I have received calls from people who thought they did things correctly, but it turned out they did not and then did not have the necessary rights secured to be able to take the action they sought. I have also received calls from inexperienced attorneys asking me for help in addressing issues they created that could have been avoided.

Nonlawyer services are generally trademark filing services and can only provide basic information related to filing applications;

they cannot provide legal guidance. Nonlawyer companies often look very official and could easily appear to offer the same level of services that are provided by lawyers; however, unless they have a licensed attorney, they cannot do so.

ARE YOU EXPOSED?

At this point, you may be wondering whether you have taken the necessary steps to protect your brand assets. If you find you have made one of the mistakes mentioned above, do not panic. Rather, be grateful and happy that you recognized your mistake and caught it sooner versus later so you can run damage control and take steps to correct potential issues as soon as possible.

Now that you have the above information, you have some choices to make. You can choose to do nothing, which I do not recommend, because the risk of doing nothing can be high. You can attempt to correct any mistakes yourself or turn to a nonlawyer service, which, again, I do not recommend. Or you can choose to engage a brand protection attorney and ask for help. No matter where you are in the brand protection process, an experienced attorney will be able to review and discuss your concerns, provide options for next steps to take, advise on how to specifically correct any issues, and evaluate with you what additional protections should be put into place to protect your brand. As Benjamin Franklin said, "An ounce of prevention is worth a pound of cure."[6] Or stated another way, it is better to be safe than sorry!

PIVOT SOONER VERSUS LATER

It is always a good idea to pivot sooner versus later to minimize risk. By writing this book, my intention is to help you identify and avoid making the same common mistakes I have seen many business owners make over the years. As I mentioned earlier, none of us are immune from making mistakes, especially when we are unfamiliar with the many intricacies that come with establishing and running a business. I include myself in this category. Before going to law school, I was involved in setting up two companies. This included creating the company names and the company logos, a creative process that I thoroughly enjoyed. The companies were named City Machinery—a metal-making machinery company—and International Food Brokers—a brokerage company that imported and exported food products and other goods.

When I set up these companies, however, I did not know the information contained in this book. I can also say that at the time I was establishing these companies, the thought of whether or not to obtain federally registered trademarks was not even something that crossed my mind. Notably, what I later came to learn is that these company names were "weak" marks, and unless we had been able to establish secondary meaning for City Machinery, the USPTO most likely would have rejected this brand name as a federally registerable word mark on the Principal Register (see chapter five for a discussion on principal versus supplemental registers). As for the mark International Food Brokers, the USPTO likely would have entirely rejected federal registration for this name because it is merely descriptive of the services the company provided. However, the logo versions for both company names may have been registrable because each was distinctive.

If you need to pivot because you hit the proverbial brick wall like I did (story to follow), there are good reasons to do so sooner versus later. The longer you use a trademark that will ultimately need to be changed, the more time and money you waste because you may need to reinvent the wheel and reinvest in marketing and advertising to rebrand rather than continuing to build on the momentum of the brand you have been using. The need to pivot away from a brand name you have created and come to love often comes with an emotional charge, since many people (including myself) get invested in and attached to their brand name. Because of this, before you fall in love with your brand name, I strongly suggest you do the necessary research and investigation to make sure that you can protect the name that you are using or intend to use. Remember to always search before you leap!

While my story about hitting a brick wall did not relate to a trademark issue, it did relate to the timing of when I went to law school. When I started International Food Brokers with my business partner, we were attending the University of Miami. We had tremendous success and brokered all kinds of products, which we sold and shipped to customers internationally in 20 ft. and 40 ft. containers.

As part of this process, we provided purchase orders to our customers stating the timing of payments. Long story short, we had a container of goods shipped to the port in Kobe, Japan, but our customer was late in making the final payment. We repeatedly explained to the customer that he would forfeit the moneys paid if the final payment was not paid right away. The customer ignored the purchase order and failed to pay in a timely manner.

Around the same time, my business partner and I went to eat a late lunch at a fast-food restaurant near the University of Miami. We took our food and sat toward the back of the restaurant where we were not in view of the people who were working there. We were engaged in talking and eating our meal. As I put a french fry in my mouth and looked down at the food in front of me, I saw out of the corner of my left eye a more than six-foot-tall, physically fit man wearing black sweatpants, a black sweatshirt, a black baseball cap, and mirror reflective sunglasses appear at the side of our table. I looked up and froze.

This incredibly ominous man reported that he had been following us for days and had a message to deliver from the customer whose payments were forfeited. "You better make the situation right or else," he said and then left the restaurant. OMG! We looked at each other in shock, our appetites gone. Virtually speechless, we left the restaurant totally freaked out. We were scared. At that point, I decided I was done with the import-export business, and it was time to pivot and focus on going to law school instead of building International Food Brokers, which seemed very risky to me. P.S., we resolved the situation by putting the buyer in touch with the seller, and they worked things out.

I am certainly not suggesting that you pivot to law school if you hit a brick wall with your trademark search. I had always planned on going to law school, just not at the time I pivoted. Instead, what I am suggesting is that it is important for you to investigate and do your due diligence sooner rather than later so that if you need to pivot your business by changing its name, logo, slogan, et cetera, you are able to do so effectively and efficiently. By being proactive, you can plan accordingly, which may save you valuable time and money and perhaps even spare you from experiencing unnecessary aggravation down the road.

In the next chapter, we will explore what can happen if you end up using a brand name similar to another company's brand name, including the risks, heartache, and potential liability that can arise as a result of trademark infringement, which can be substantial.

CHAPTER 3

Risks of Using a Brand Name Similar to Another Company's Brand Name

I<small>F YOU CREATE A COMPANY NAME, LOGO, OR TAGLINE TO SELL</small> your goods or services and you do not do a preliminary screening (to be discussed in greater detail in chapter seven), you are potentially putting your company at risk of being accused of infringing another company's trademark rights.

You may be wondering how an infringement situation will be brought to your attention. Well, one way you may know is if a company that believes you are infringing its rights serves you with a notice that it has filed a lawsuit against you. This is an aggressive approach some companies use to enforce their rights, and such notices generally come without any warning, which can be quite alarming. Another approach companies use is to send you a very serious letter (commonly referred to as a cease and desist or demand letter) wherein the company puts you on notice and outlines the reasons why it believes your mark is infringing upon its rights. Cease and desist letters also commonly demand the alleged infringing party immediately stop using the marks at issue. Some cease and desist letters also include a demand for payment to resolve the matter or may request the alleged infringing party turn over sales information relating to the goods or services that have been sold using the allegedly infringing mark. Sales information can be used to determine the amount of profit that was gained from the infringement and what amount of money will be required to resolve the matter.

If you or your company ever receives either a notice of lawsuit or a cease and desist letter, these should be taken very seriously. In this regard, the best practice and most prudent course of action is to engage an attorney as soon as possible to review and analyze these documents and help you determine an action plan to appropriately respond. It is important to note that a company that has a federally registered trademark will generally be in a much stronger position to file a lawsuit or issue a demand letter against an alleged infringer compared to a company that does not own a registered mark or that merely has common law rights.

DO NOT IGNORE A CEASE AND DESIST LETTER

Do not ignore a cease and desist letter. Cease and desist letters should be taken very seriously. In my experience, when these letters are ignored, it generally does not play out well for the company or person receiving the letter. In fact, if a company's principal ignores a cease and desist letter, they are at a higher risk of being found personally liable for the infringement. That said, irrespective of whether a corporate officer or director ignores the cease and desist letter, they can be held personally liable for the trademark infringement committed by their company. In my experience, many company principals are not aware of this exposure and, unfortunately, may feel a false sense of security, thinking that by operating under a corporate entity or as a limited liability company, they are shielded from personal liability. However, this is not always the case—there is substantial risk. If another company is successful in proving trademark infringement and the company's principals are found personally liable, a monetary judgment could be entered against them, exposing their personal assets. This means that their personal assets are at risk of being forfeited to satisfy the judgment.

TRADEMARK INFRINGEMENT CAN RESULT IN LARGE MONETARY DAMAGES AND PRISON TIME

A company's principal may also be found criminally liable if the company continues to use the trademark after receipt of a cease and desist letter or after the court enters an injunction to stop the infringing conduct. Ignoring a court order is a very serious matter and can result in the parties involved being found in contempt of court, which, depending on the circumstances of the case, could result in prison time. The Trademark Counterfeiting Act provides felony criminal penalties in the most egregious type of trademark infringement cases, that is, the use of an identical trademark for the same goods or services registered with the USPTO.[7] An example of a counterfeit trademark case is when a retailer sells knockoff Louis Vuitton handbags with the LV logo that reflects the identical trademark registered with the USPTO by Louis Vuitton's parent company.

Early on in my practice, I was involved in a case where a woman who had no prior criminal record was accused of trademark infringement by several luxury brands for selling knockoff handbags. She was arrested. The prosecutor sought jail time and millions of dollars in restitution damages for the benefit of the brand owners. Although this client was found liable, the trial team was successful in reducing her penalty to probation, which included having her passport taken away and the payment of restitution damages in the range of hundreds of thousands of dollars. This was a good result for the client under the circumstances.

Penalties for counterfeit trademarks are significant and can result in monetary fines up to $30 million as well as jail time up to life in prison if death occurs as a result of the counterfeiting.[8] For a first violation, the monetary fines may be as high as $5 million, and there may be up to ten years of jail time.[9] For subsequent violations as well as for first violations where the counterfeiter causes serious bodily injury or where the counterfeiting involves military goods or services or counterfeit drugs, the monetary damages may be as high as $15 million, and there may be up to 20 years of jail time.[10] For subsequent offenses involving counterfeit military goods or services or counterfeit drugs, the monetary fines increase to up to $30 million and the prison time to up to 30 years.[11] Where death is caused as a result of the counterfeiting, an individual can be imprisoned for up to life.[12] It should be noted that, if one is found liable, penalties can include a monetary fine as well as prison time. Trademark infringement is considered an aggravated felony under federal law.[13]

HIRE AN ATTORNEY TO RESPOND TO OR SEND A CEASE AND DESIST LETTER

It is generally best to have an experienced trademark attorney respond on your behalf to a cease and desist letter as opposed to responding without guidance. What is said to the other side can impact your case in negative ways, and an experienced attorney will be able to assist you in navigating the situation so that what you say does not backfire.

Also, in my experience, a cease and desist letter sent by a trademark attorney on the company's behalf carries more weight and signals to the alleged infringer that the company is taking the matter seriously. Significantly, the company seeking to enforce its rights by sending the cease and desist letter needs to be sure that the letter is carefully tailored to assert its trademark rights while also avoiding misstating or mischaracterizing issues that could backfire and create possible defenses or, worse, prompt a countersuit or declaratory judgment lawsuit in response. A declaratory judgment lawsuit is a type of proceeding wherein a party seeks a judge to declare the legal rights between the parties in a matter before the court. For example, where there is a trademark dispute, a party asks a judge to decide which party has the superior trademark rights.

Sending a cease and desist letter to a company that is located outside of your jurisdiction (the state where your business is located) could result in your company being sued in that other jurisdiction, which in addition to being inconvenient, often results in the litigation being more expensive. By sending a cease and desist letter, the trademark owner exposes their company or themselves to, at minimum, a declaratory judgment lawsuit being filed in the jurisdiction where the alleged infringer resides. This becomes a race to the courthouse because the accused infringer does not want to end up being sued in a different jurisdiction.

A trademark litigation attorney will be able to do the necessary research and analysis to determine the best approach under the circumstances and will be able to assist you with scrutinizing the situation and verifying whether you would be deemed the senior user so that your accusation does not backfire. Unfortunately, I have seen situations where someone believes their mark is being infringed, and then they learn that the alleged infringer was an earlier user of the mark with superior common law rights.

Also, when you accuse someone of infringement, it is important to have all your proverbial ducks in a row because alleged infringers often come out with guns blazing and will look at all options available to them to invalidate the trademark. It is reasonable to expect that the company receiving the cease and desist letter may claim that you have no trademark rights for various reasons, including naked licensing (discussed in chapter one) and nonuse of the mark as well as registration deficiencies or irregularities (discussed in chapter 11).

There are also strategic considerations when sending a demand letter. For example, it is important to consider the impact on your business if the demand letter is shared and goes viral. It is important that the tone of the letter be in line with the offense and not over the top.

Generally, courts will not allow the same action to proceed in more than one jurisdiction. When an action between the same parties related to the same underlying facts is filed in more than one jurisdiction, in my experience, the parties file motions in court arguing why the litigation should proceed in one jurisdiction over another jurisdiction. The judge presiding over the case will then consider the arguments made by each side, apply the relevant law, and enter an order resolving the jurisdictional dispute. Jurisdictional disputes are time-intensive and expensive, adding potentially thousands of dollars to the cost of the litigation. Preference is generally given to the location where the case was first filed, assuming the court has jurisdiction over the matter.

Also, in my experience, it is not a good idea for a trademark owner to directly address the situation with the infringer. You can say something that is taken out of context, and it can backfire on you. With the buffer of an attorney, you are protected from a situation like this.

TRADEMARK INFRINGEMENT CAN LEAD TO
COSTLY AND DISRUPTIVE REBRANDING

A company accused of infringement may need to stop using its current brand identity and come up with a new name, logo, or slogan. This process can be expensive and time-consuming, as rebranding requires the creation of new marketing materials. The longer a company has been in business, the more difficult rebranding becomes from a customer perspective. Customers as well as employees may have a strong emotional attachment to an old brand identity, and the sudden change may be confusing and disruptive. It may take time for customers and employees to adjust to a new brand. Thus, it is important for every business to do its due diligence and ensure it is not infringing on another company's intellectual property before launching a new brand identity. If a rebrand is necessary, a resolution can be structured so that the rebrand is not as disruptive as it otherwise might be if the terms were not finessed. For example, I have been successful in negotiating a rebrand over time as opposed to an immediate halt. This (in some instances) allowed the accused infringer time to sell off its remaining inventory and roll out a rebrand over several months.

An example of how trademark infringement can play out and result in the need for rebranding occurred in the *Starbucks Corporation v. Lundberg* case, where Starbucks sued Samantha Lundberg, the owner of a coffee shop in Oregon who changed its name from Astoria Coffeehouse to Sambuck's Coffeehouse.[14] After learning of the coffee shop, Starbucks sent a cease and desist letter to Ms. Lundberg asserting infringement of its trademark and requesting she discontinue use of the name. When she refused to give up her small business's name, Starbucks filed a lawsuit against her for trademark infringement and trademark dilution.

Ms. Lundberg claimed that she named the company Sambuck's because her maiden name was Buck. However, the Oregon District Court found that when Ms. Lundberg opened the shop under the Sambuck's name, she was already aware of Starbucks and had been to the popular coffee house herself.[15] The Court concluded that Sambuck's was likely to dilute the Starbucks mark.[16] The Starbucks trademark was found to be sufficiently distinctive, and survey evidence showed that the Sambuck's mark caused an association in consumer's minds with the Starbucks mark.[17] Further, the Court found that the Sambuck's name infringed on Starbucks' federally registered mark because it was likely to cause consumer confusion.[18] Based on expert testimony and surveys submitted by the parties, the Court was able to conclude that the "Sambuck's" mark would cause initial interest confusion because the marks were so alike, and consumers would be led to believe that Ms. Lundberg's coffee house was associated or affiliated with Starbucks in some way.[19]

The Court ordered a permanent injunction, preventing Ms. Lundberg from using the Sambuck's mark or any other variation that might resemble a Starbucks trademark.[20] Because of this injunction, Ms. Lundberg was required to completely rebrand her coffee shop and change all marketing, signage, and materials that had the Sambuck's name. Ms. Lundberg said herself that she "[threw] away thousands of dollars worth of stuff . . . and [was] left paying thousands of dollars more to have new things made."[21] As the dispute revealed, Ms. Lundberg would have been better off not altering the name of the coffee shop and continuing to operate as Astoria Coffeehouse. This is an example of a "good idea" backfiring.

Another example where rebranding was required occurred in the *World Wildlife Fund v. World Wrestling Federation* case related to the mark WWF. This case was filed in the United Kingdom most likely because it was the jurisdiction of the earliest use of the mark WWF. The World of Wrestling Federation (the "Federation") registered the WWF mark in the 1980s, however, the World Wildlife Fund (the "Fund") had already registered the mark in 1961.[22] After a lengthy legal battle between the two of them, the parties entered into a settlement agreement in 1994 that restricted the Federation's ability to use the WWF mark in trade and marketing.[23] However, in 2002, the Fund filed a lawsuit for breach of contract, claiming that the Federation had breached the terms of the agreement when it registered the domain name "www.WWF.com."[24] The England and Wales Court of Appeal (Civil Division) ruled in favor of the Fund, stating, "If the Federation wanted to develop a worldwide trade, whether through the internet or any other means, the letters WWF were a very risky base on which to build it. When it established its website, it was, or should have been, fully aware of that fact. The costs of rebranding now, after some five years of development, are entirely attributable to its own decision to take that risk."[25] In the end, the Federation was forced to rebrand its enterprise and began using the acronym WWE for World of Wrestling Entertainment rather than WWF. The exact cost of this rebrand is not known, but many speculate that it was very expensive for the Federation considering how well known the brand was as WWF.

The cost of rebranding can be devasting to a business depending on the size of the business and how long it has been in operation. Generally, the cost of rebranding increases as time passes. The longer the company has been in business, the more likely there will be more marketing and promotional material that needs to be rebranded. Therefore, the sooner a company becomes aware of the need to rebrand, the sooner it should take steps to do so.

LIABILITY FOR TRADEMARK INFRINGEMENT MAY RESULT IN HAVING TO TURN OVER ALL OF YOUR PROFITS

Another potential damage that can result from trademark infringement is the disgorgement of profits. Disgorgement of profits means the infringing party may be required to turn over, or disgorge, all the profits it made from its wrongful use of the infringed trademark. For example, if a company starts using a logo that is similar to another company's well-known logo and the original company sues for trademark infringement and wins, the court may require the infringing company to pay back all the profits it made using the similar logo. The theory behind this is to correct the wrong, that is, to not allow the infringing party to benefit (without permission) from the goodwill and reputation of the company that procured legitimate trademark rights to protect its brand. As I am sure you can imagine, having to pay back all the profits made can be crippling to a business and could even lead to the need to file corporate and personal bankruptcy.

Disgorgement of profits was awarded in the *Romag Fasteners, Inc. v. Fossil Group, Inc., et al.* case.[26] The case involved handbag fasteners. Romag sells magnetic snap fasteners for use in leather products. Fossil creates, markets, and supplies a wide range of fashion products. Romag and Fossil had an agreement allowing Fossil to use Romag's fasteners in its handbags and other products. Romag learned that the factories in China hired by Fossil were using counterfeit fasteners to make the products, and Fossil was not sufficiently guarding against the Chinese factories doing so. This case went all the way to the United States Supreme Court.

As a result of the *Romag* case, the Supreme Court made it easier for an aggrieved party to recover the infringer's profits. In particular, the Supreme Court held that although willfulness is an important factor for the court to consider in awarding damages, it is not necessary to prove that the trademark infringement was willful to be able to recover the infringer's profits. Thus, even if a party did not intentionally infringe, it can still be liable for turning over the profits that it made when infringement is found.

TRADEMARK LITIGATION IS VERY EXPENSIVE

When you are considering whether to engage in certain risky behavior related to your branding, it is important to be aware of the incredible expense associated with litigation. By risky behavior, I mean moving forward with branding strategies without doing the necessary research to make sure you will not be infringing on someone else's trademark rights. It has been my experience that many businesses do not set aside much money to protect their IP assets, let alone the significant amount of reserve funds that will be required on that "rainy day" when the company may become entangled in litigation. As a result, most businesses are not at all prepared for the financial stress that the cost of litigation will have on their cash flows and overall operating budgets. In both federal and state courts in Florida (and other states), a corporate entity must be represented by an attorney in court and cannot represent itself through a nonattorney. Hiring an attorney, especially an intellectual property litigation attorney, can become extremely expensive. Further, not only is litigation expensive, it is also risky because there are no guarantees that you will be able to achieve the desired end result.

The American Intellectual Property Law Association (AIPLA) compiles an economic report every couple of years that includes information on costs associated with trademark litigation. To give you an idea of the associated costs, the AIPLA 2023 Report of the Economic Survey outlines various factors that impact the cost of litigation and states the average cost of litigation will vary depending on the amount of damages claimed in the case.[27] For example, when there is less than $1 million at stake, the average cost for a trademark litigation case, including pretrial, trial, posttrial, and appellate fees (when applicable), is $542,000. When there is $1 million to $10 million at stake, the average cost is $999,000. For matters with damages between $10 million and $25 million, the average cost is $1,703,000. When the amount at issue is greater than $25 million, the average cost for trademark infringement litigation is $2,628,000.

Various factors influence the cost of litigation being higher or lower than the average. Some of these factors are the contentiousness of the parties or their attorneys. If the parties empower their attorneys to fight over everything, numerous motions will be filed and responded to, and evidentiary hearings will be required, all of which will dramatically increase legal fees. In addition, some cases require more witnesses than other cases, which will also likely result in higher legal fees because of the time involved in preparing for and taking depositions and then reviewing and analyzing the transcripts to build the case.

In my experience, most lawyers will not agree to handle a trademark litigation matter on a contingency fee basis (meaning, agreeing to wait on payment of legal fees and only getting paid when the litigation is over and their client is awarded monetary damages or a settlement is reached involving the payment of money). Instead, they require payment of monthly invoices and very often require a monetary retainer for anticipated upcoming legal fees, which they apply to outstanding invoices or hold in reserve as security and then require the client pay invoices when they become due as the case moves along.

So, as you can see, the cost of litigation is substantial. Whether or not you ultimately choose to act cautiously is a personal decision that often rides on a business owner's stomach for risk. If you are going to engage in risky behavior, it is a good idea to have a rainy-day litigation fund or resources available in case you are sued. Frankly, the more successful a business becomes and the more recognizable the business's brand identity is, the more reason there is to be proactive in maintaining a reserve account in the event resources are needed later to fund litigation to protect its brand.

In addition to its high cost, litigation will also disrupt your company's day-to-day business operations due to time spent focusing on the litigation instead of growing your business. Further, litigation is also likely to take an emotional toll on those directly involved with the case. While most cases tend to resolve before they go to trial, the overall process can become unpredictable. Unfortunately, despite all of this, it may be necessary at times for a company to file a lawsuit to get the infringing company to take the matter seriously.

INSURANCE FOR INTELLECTUAL PROPERTY INFRINGEMENT CLAIMS

Because IP infringement claims can put your business at financial risk, it is important to secure (or at least consider securing) commercial insurance to help protect your business from infringement claims. Insurance coverage for copyright infringement claims brought against your business is commonly found in commercial general liability insurance policies. Note, however, that many insurance policies only cover unintentional infringement claims. In addition, you can purchase IP protection insurance that may specifically cover the enforcement and defense of intellectual property infringement of patents, trademarks, and copyrights, depending on the policy purchased. If the matter is covered, insurance can help with attorneys' fees, settlement payments, and payments to satisfy judgments up to the policy limits. Some policies may even help pay costs to pursue infringement claims. The cost for this type of insurance varies based on different factors, including the location of the company, type of business, and revenue. Insurance is higher in some states than in other states. It is best to speak with and be guided by an experienced and reputable insurance agent who can provide you with insurance options and a quote for IP protection coverage.

If you are accused of intellectual property infringement (for example, you receive a cease and desist letter asserting infringement), you should review your insurance policies to see if you have insurance coverage and what the requirements are to put your insurance company on notice. Commercial general liability insurance policies might cover "advertising injury liability," which may include a trademark infringement claim. In this regard, consulting with an experienced insurance agent along with a knowledgeable IP attorney, in conjunction with an insurance attorney, to review your insurance policies to understand the scope of coverage is prudent.

Your best insurance is to be proactive and try to avoid issues before they arise. You can do this by enlisting the help of, and working with, experienced professionals who can guide you and give you peace of mind. Although I have already addressed the significance of trademark infringement and used the phrase IP (the commonly used abbreviation for intellectual property), in the following chapter, I will outline the four general types of intellectual property and explain in more detail how you can determine what IP assets you have.

CHAPTER 4

Types of Intellectual Property

INTELLECTUAL PROPERTY REFERS TO CREATIONS OF THE MIND. Unlike tangible property (that is, currency, real estate, physical things, et cetera), intellectual property is an "intangible asset," meaning you cannot physically touch it. In this chapter, I will discuss the four types of IP individuals and businesses create and go to great lengths to protect.

There are four general types of intellectual property:

- Trademarks
- Copyrights
- Patents
- Trade Secrets

TRADEMARKS

A trademark is a word, symbol, logo, design, slogan, or combination of these elements that identifies and distinguishes the goods or services of one company from those of other companies. In other words, a trademark is a unique identifier that is used to represent a particular brand, product, or service. Trademarks prevent confusion among consumers as to the source of the goods or services and provide legal protection for a brand, including a company's goodwill and reputation. "Goodwill" relates to the inherent value of the trademark, meaning the extra value that the trademark generates due to its recognition among consumers. In chapter five, I will address and provide examples of different types of trademarks.

A trademark that relates to a company's services versus its goods can be referred to as a service mark. Oftentimes, although the mark relates to services instead of goods, it is still referred to as a trademark. Trademarks will be addressed in greater detail in the remaining chapters of this book.

COPYRIGHTS

A copyright gives the creator of an original work the exclusive right to make commercial use of the work, such as printing, publishing, performing, recording, or licensing the work to others. The word "work" is used to refer to the item created. A copyright is created at the time the work is created. It is a type of intellectual property that protects original works of authorship as soon as an author fixes the work in a tangible form of expression. For example, this book is protected by copyright, which is reflected at the beginning of the book as follows: "© 2024 L.A. Perkins. All rights reserved." The phrase "all rights reserved" is not a U.S. requirement, but there is no harm in including it for clarity. It means the copyright holder reserves all rights and no one may use the work without the copyright holder's permission.

How long does copyright protection last? Generally, if the work was created on or after January 1, 1978, copyright protection lasts for the life of the author plus an additional 70 years after the author's death.[28] If the work is a joint work with multiple authors, the duration of the copyright lasts for 70 years after the last surviving author's death. For works that are anonymous, pseudonymous, or made for hire, the copyright lasts for a term of 95 years from the year of its publication or a term of 120 years from the year of its creation, whichever expires first.[29] For works created before January 1, 1978, that were not published or registered as of that date, the duration of the copyright is generally the same as for works created on or after January 1, 1978.[30] For works created and published or registered before 1978, the duration of the copyright protection is up to 95 years.[31]

Unlike trademarks, where registration is required to use the ® symbol, when a work is created, the copyright owner of the work may use the © symbol within it to put others on notice that copyright ownership and protection are claimed.

If someone seeks to register a copyright in the United States, registration is done through the U.S. Copyright Office. Examples of copyrightable works include:[32]

- Literary works, including computer programs
- Musical works, including any accompanying words
- Dramatic works, including any accompanying music
- Pantomimes and choreographic works
- Pictorial, graphic, and sculptural works, including maps and technical drawings
- Motion pictures and other audiovisual works
- Sound recordings, which are works that result from the fixation of a series of musical, spoken, or other sounds
- Architectural works

There are benefits to obtaining a copyright registration. If a copyright registration is obtained (not all works are approved for copyright registration), it establishes an official record and date of the copyright and can be very useful in prosecuting or defending a claim of copyright infringement. Works that are deemed insufficiently creative are not approved for registration. For example, copyright does not protect:[33]

- Ideas, procedures, methods, systems, processes, concepts, principles, or discoveries
- Works that are not fixed in a tangible form (such as a choreographic work that has not been notated or recorded or an improvisational speech that has not been written down)
- Titles, names, short phrases, or slogans
- Familiar symbols or designs
- Mere variations of typographic ornamentation, lettering, or coloring
- Mere listings of ingredients or contents

Copyright infringement means someone other than the owner of the copyright has reproduced, performed, displayed, or distributed the work without the owner's permission. Creating a derivative work without permission is also copyright infringement, even if it is not sold. A derivative work is a work based on or derived from one or more already existing works. A common example of derivative work is a new, updated, or revised edition of a book.

To be able to bring a claim for copyright infringement in federal court, copyright registration is necessary. If someone has a claim for copyright infringement and they do not already have a copyright registration, a copyright registration can be applied for on an expedited basis. However, requesting a copyright registration on an expedited basis results in an extra expense because there is a surcharge for the expedited processing.

A major benefit to having a copyright registration is being able to obtain statutory damages versus having to prove actual damages when bringing a copyright infringement claim. Statutory damages are a type of damage awarded to compensate a claimant for an injury or loss if their claim is successful. The amount is pre-established by statute. Currently, in the United States, an owner of a copyright registration could be awarded statutory damages between $750 and $30,000.[34] If the copyright infringement is found to be willful, the statutory damages sum may be as high as $150,000.[35]

In my practice, I have assisted clients in bringing and defending copyright infringement claims related to unauthorized use of photographs. One common mistake people often make is thinking that if an image or photograph is used on the internet, it is fair game for them to use. This is a big mistake. Unless someone has a license to use an image or material created by another person, it is not a good idea to assume that using the image will be okay, even if you see other people using the same image. If the owner of the work learns of the unauthorized use and the work is being used commercially (for example, on a business's website or social media platform), it is very likely that either a cease and desist letter will be sent demanding the infringer immediately cease using the work and pay damages for the unauthorized use, or the alleged infringer may be served with a lawsuit as the first notice of the alleged infringement.

Street Art
Under copyright law, even though graffiti is illegal when it is created without permission from the owner of the surface, the creator of the work still owns the copyright to the graffiti art design that

the artist created on the surface. I was involved in a case where a street artist who had permission to paint a beautiful image on the side of a building in Miami asserted a copyright infringement claim against a car dealer for advertising a photo of the car it was selling with the street art in the background. The car dealership did not get the street artist's permission before using their work in the dealership advertising.

Logos

It often makes sense to file a copyright application for a logo design for which a trademark registration is sought. Many brands have done so. For example, Louis Vuitton has obtained trademark protection and copyright protection for its Toile Monogram design mark (U.S. Trademark Reg. Nos, 1770131, 1875198, 2399161, and 4192541) and its black Multicolor Monogram print (U.S. Copyright Reg. No. VA-1-250-121 and U.S. Copyright Supp. Reg. No. VA-1-365-644), respectively.

Generally, it is in a company's best interest to make sure it owns all the work created by employees as well as contractors who do work for the company. Thus, I regularly counsel clients to have employees and contractors sign work-for-hire agreements. A work-for-hire agreement makes clear that the individual or entity who is doing work for a company (for example, a website developer) agrees that they claim no ownership rights in what they are creating for the company or employer and that all the rights are owned by the company or employer.

Artificial Intelligence

You may be wondering whether you could hold a copyright for content created using artificial intelligence (AI) programs. This is a hot topic due to the widespread use of these programs. In 2022, a copyright claimant, Stephen Thaler, filed a lawsuit challenging the U.S. Copyright Office's denial of his copyright application to register a particular visual artwork that he claimed was generated entirely by an AI program.[36] Contrary to Dr. Thaler's argument that human authorship is not required by the Copyright Act, the federal district court disagreed. The federal court held that "human authorship is an essential part of a valid copyright claim"[37] because only human authors need copyright protection as an incentive to create works. However, the federal court did not consider or rule upon whether the result would be different based on a copyright claimant's involvement in the generative process by prompting the AI program because that issue was not before the court. Although the court did not rule on this issue, the U.S. Copyright Office has issued guidance on the topic indicating that it would be unlikely to find the required human authorship if a work was generated by an AI program in response to text prompts. Rather, for the U.S. Copyright Office to grant a copyright registration, there must be sufficient human involvement in the authorship of the work.[38] The law is rapidly evolving as it relates to copyright protection for AI generated work and should be closely monitored.

PATENTS

If you have invented or created something unique, it may be protectable under patent law. Before we get into the types of patents, I want to make sure you are aware of two very important points that could impact your ability to obtain a patent (assuming you have a patentable invention).

First to File

The first important point for you to know is that the inventor who first files their patent application with the USPTO receives priority in the application process for filing first. However, filing a patent application does not necessarily mean that the patent will be approved, and the patent registration date is distinct from the filing date. Up until 2013, when the America Invents Act became effective, the inventor who first created the invention received priority in obtaining a U.S. patent.[39] After 2013, the inventor who first files for a patent receives priority in obtaining a U.S. patent. The priority date is important because the inventor with the earliest filed patent application wins the race to the rights to the patent.

One-Year Application Filing Deadline

The second important point for you to know is the requirement that a patent application must be filed within one year of public disclosure of the invention. Thus, it is extremely important to act with urgency to protect your rights. Failing to do so can result in being precluded from obtaining patent protection on your amazing, novel invention. Unfortunately, because this scenario occurs far too often, I highly recommend that you consult with an intellectual property attorney sooner rather than later so that you are not blindsided.

There are four types of patent applications:

- Provisional patents
- Design patents
- Utility patents
- Plant patents

Provisional Patents

One way to win the race to have the earliest filing date is to file a provisional patent application with the USPTO. A provisional patent application does not itself become an issued patent, and it does not start the patent term clock. A provisional application is a lower-cost patent filing. Such an application may be filed without formal patent claims, an oath, or a declaration. It requires describing the invention as completely as possible. Once a provisional application is filed, the term "patent pending" may be used in connection with the description of the invention.

The provisional patent application has a pendency of only 12 months from the date it was filed. Thus, an applicant must file a nonprovisional patent application within 12 months of filing the provisional patent application. Only in extraordinary circumstances and for a hefty fee can an applicant get an extra two months if the 12-month filing deadline is missed.

A provisional patent application provides an applicant with peace of mind in having an early filing date on the invention while allowing more time to continue working on the invention.

Design and Utility Patents

Simply put, a design patent protects the way a product looks, whereas a utility patent protects the way a product works and functions. Generally, design patents are less expensive and can be obtained faster than utility patents. The primary benefit of a utility patent is that it provides broad protection. By comparison, design patents have a narrower scope of protection. A design patent protects only certain, limited features as specified in the patent. However, its protection is very important if the main features of the product are aesthetic. Multiple design patents can be applied for relating to the same product. Notably, it is possible to get both a design and utility patent on the same item; however, to do so would require separate patent applications with individual fees.

The average design patent approval rate from 2011 through 2020 was 69.2 percent, while the average utility patent approval rate for the same time period was 51.4 percent.[40]

Although design patents do not provide the broad protection of a utility patent, they can still supply significant protection in a court of law. For example, in 2017, Apple was awarded substantial damages in a suit against Samsung wherein Apple sued Samsung for infringing design and utility patents related to its smartphone. Apple claimed that three design patents were infringed: (1) the D618,677 patent, covering a black rectangular front face of a phone with rounded corners; (2) the D593,087 patent, covering a rectangular front face of a phone with rounded corners and a raised rim; and (3) the D604,305 patent, covering a grid of 16 colorful icons on a black screen.[41]

After extensive litigation, including a retrial, a California jury awarded $399 million in damages to Apple for Samsung's design patent infringement, representing all the profits Samsung made from its infringing smartphones.[42] Samsung appealed the decision to the U.S. Supreme Court, and the Court returned the case back to the trial court to determine whether the damage award should stand or if a new damages trial was required based on the U.S. Supreme Court's rulings on the law. The trial court ultimately entered an order requiring a new trial on the design patent damages based on an error in the jury instruction on damages.[43] Based upon a review of the trial court's docket, on June 27, 2018, the parties filed a Joint Notice of Settlement and Stipulation of Dismissal with Prejudice, advising the Court "that they have agreed to drop and settle their remaining claims and counterclaims in this matter."[44] The terms of the settlement are not part of the court record and are likely confidential.

Plant Patents

A plant patent is granted for newly invented plant varieties of asexually produced plants. The plant must be asexually propagated to be patentable. This means the plants must reproduce by means other than seeds. Plants cultivated using tubers and wild or uncultivated plants are not patentable. Tuber plants are high in starch. Examples are potatoes, yams, and taro. Wild plants are untended by humans; they evolve in the wild. If a plant is in a location where humans did not intend for it to be, it is deemed uncultivated.[45]

A registered patent protects the patent owner's right to exclude others from asexually reproducing the plant and using, offering to sell, or selling the plant so produced or any of its parts throughout the United States. In recent years, the USPTO has issued patents for certain cannabis plants.

To be candid, plant patents seem nebulous and scientific to me. Like with other types of patents, when my clients seek patent protection for plants, I collaborate with patent attorneys who are versed in the specific science involved and able to prepare patent applications for them. A patent attorney is required to have a science background and pass a Patent Bar Examination to represent inventors before the United States Patent Office.

How Long Does a Patent Last?

The patent term for a design patent application filed on or after May 13, 2015, has a term of 15 years from the date the patent was granted. If the design patent application was filed prior to May 13, 2015, then the term is 14 years from the date the patent was granted.[46]

The patent term for a utility or plant patent begins on the date the patent is issued and ends 20 years from the date on which the patent application was filed in the United States or, if the application contains reference to an earlier-filed application, 20 years from the date when the earliest application was filed.[47]

TRADE SECRETS

A trade secret can be any form or type of "financial, business, scientific, technical, economic, or engineering information, including patterns, plans, compilations, program devices, formulas, designs, prototypes, methods, techniques, processes, procedures, programs, or codes, whether tangible or intangible, and whether or how stored, compiled, or memorialized physically, electronically, graphically, photographically, or in writing."[48] For something to be deemed a trade secret, the following three elements are necessary: First, the information must have either actual or potential independent economic value by virtue of not being generally known. Second, the information must have value to others who cannot legitimately obtain the information. Third, the information must be subject to reasonable efforts to maintain its secrecy.

To maintain a trade secret, the information should be shared on a need-to-know basis only. For example, if you have a secret formula for a product, it is likely that not all of your employees need to know the formula. If this is the case and you share the information with all your employees, trade secret protection is jeopardized. This means a court might find that by allowing employees who did not "need to know" the details of your secret formula access to the information, you did not engage in sufficient reasonable efforts to maintain the "secrecy" of the formula. One tool used to maintain secrecy is to limit and monitor employee access to research and development information, sensitive files, and access to laboratories. Another tool for maintaining secrecy is the use of confidentiality and noncompete agreements. Cyber-security measures should also be considered and put in place to protect trade secrets.

When I think of examples of trade secrets, the first thing that comes to my mind is the Coca-Cola formula, which is kept a secret and locked in a vault. Only the general ingredients are disclosed by Coca-Cola, that is, carbonated water, high-fructose corn syrup, caramel color, phosphoric acid, natural flavors, and caffeine.[49] There is much speculation as to the "natural flavors," but that information, along with the quantities of ingredients used, is kept a secret. The Food and Drug Administration requires that only ingredients that are more than 2 percent of the product must be listed, in descending order by weight.[50] Incidental additives, which have no technical or functional effect, are exempt from labeling.[51] Spices, natural flavors, and artificial flavors may be generically declared as such.[52]

While in Atlanta visiting family, I visited the World of Coca-Cola Museum and saw the outside of the guarded vault where the secret formula is kept. To this day, Coca-Cola maintains "the recipe is one of the most closely guarded secrets of all time."[53]

I have handled theft of trade secret cases, and I have worked with clients to identify, review, and implement proper controls within their businesses to protect their trade secrets. In my experience, the companies who were proactive and took steps to protect their trade secrets were in a much better position to obtain an injunction precluding former employees from using stolen trade secret information.

HOW TO IDENTIFY WHAT IP YOU HAVE

Before you can take steps to protect your IP assets, you must first identify what IP assets you have. The above explanations will hopefully get you thinking in a general sense about what IP assets you may have that need protection. However, the best way for you to make sure you are aware of your IP assets and how to protect them is to engage an intellectual property attorney who can help identify IP assets by conducting what I call an "IP audit," make a plan of action, and prioritize what needs to be done.

IP Audit

When a client engages my firm to conduct an IP audit, I first talk with them to get an overview of their company and determine the scope of the audit. Next, I provide my client with a proprietary audit form to complete and return to my office. The form includes numerous questions related to marketing content, legal documents in place, products or services sold, additional products or services they intend to sell, processes, status of all copyrights, and trademark and patent protection, as well as searches and opinions related thereto and expansion plans. After the client returns the audit form to me, I review the information and meet with them to do a deeper dive into their business. During this meeting, I ask more specific questions about their IP and their business objectives. Following this, depending on the scope of the client engagement, I then prepare a written report outlining action steps to protect their IP ownership rights.

My intention is that, by reading up to this point in the book, you now have a general understanding of the different types of intellectual property and how you can determine what IP you have. The information provided is not comprehensive, and there are many nuances that may have an impact on the available protections.

While I briefly discussed what a trademark is in this chapter, in the next chapter, I will explain trademarks in greater detail, including explaining the difference between common law trademark rights and the rights obtained through federal registration of a trademark or service mark with the USPTO. I will also touch upon the difference between federal registration and state registration rights obtained by registering a trademark in an individual state where a company conducts its business.

CHAPTER 5

Trademark Fundamentals

I N T H I S C H A P T E R , I D I S C U S S T R A D E M A R K S I N G R E A T E R D E T A I L and provide examples of the different types, which will help you identify your current trademarks and the type of branding that will enable you to obtain trademark protection. As stated previously, a trademark is a type of intellectual property. It is often one of the most important assets a company has. A memorable and distinctive trademark is extremely helpful in cultivating brand awareness and important for a company to be able to distinguish its goods or services from a competing company's goods or services in the marketplace. A trademark indicates the source of origin such that if a consumer purchases a good or service with a certain trademark, there is an expectation as to the quality and value of what they will receive. A great example of this is McDonald's golden arches trademark. When we see the famous "golden arches" logo, we as consumers know it represents a McDonald's restaurant and understand what to expect from the fast-food dining experience. We expect consistency, no matter which McDonald's restaurant we go to in the United States.

TRADEMARK RIGHTS CAN BE TRANSFERRED

In addition to being something that can be protected through federal registration in the United States, a registered trademark is a valuable asset that can be bought, sold, licensed, or inherited. However, the transfer or licensing of a trademark must be done carefully to ensure that all the trademark protections are preserved. To do this, I again strongly recommend that you engage an attorney who, among other things, will be able to make sure that the trademarks (and other IP assets) are correctly referenced in a purchase and sale agreement, as well as assist with the necessary due diligence to make sure that the trademark rights have not been compromised and that the buyer is actually receiving the rights they believe they are purchasing.

HOW TRADEMARK RIGHTS ARE CREATED

In the United States, trademark rights can be created through common law rights and federal registration rights. Remember, I discussed common law rights in chapter one. Common law rights are the rights an individual or company obtains when a trademark is used in commerce and no state or federal registration rights are obtained. Common law rights protect the company only in the jurisdictions where the trademark is being used. For example, if a business is operating under the trademark Yummie, selling cookies only in Miami, Florida, then that business has common law trademark rights in Miami, Florida. That means if a competing company started selling cookies in Miami, Florida using the same name, the company that started using the mark first could stop the second company from using it.

On the other hand, if a business in Atlanta, Georgia, started selling cookies in Atlanta under the brand name Yummie, the Miami company's common law rights would not enable it to stop the Atlanta company from selling cookies under the brand name. However, there is an exception. If the Miami company has a website where it receives cookie orders from anywhere in the United States (including Atlanta, Georgia), the Miami company may be able to enforce its common law rights against the Atlanta company and preclude it from using the mark Yummie because the Miami company was the first to use the brand name in association with the sale of cookies.

STATE TRADEMARK REGISTRATION

Before I address federal trademark registration, I want to make you aware that trademark rights can be applied for at the state level. Each state in the United States has a process by which trademarks can be registered. This is distinct from setting up a fictitious name, which is referred to as a doing business as (d/b/a) name. Typically, to apply for a state trademark registration, you need to already be using the mark in commerce. Requirements vary from state to state; however, federal trademark rights supersede state trademark rights, and it is not necessary to obtain a state trademark registration if you have obtained a federal trademark registration. Registering a trademark at the state level provides minimal protection; it does not provide as much protection as a federal trademark registration.

However, if a company does not meet the requirements of federal registration (addressed in chapter six), registering a trademark at the state level does provide some benefits. State registration puts other companies on notice that you are claiming trademark rights for a particular mark, and the registration will likely come up in a state trademark search (searches are addressed in chapter seven), which could dissuade others from using the same or similar mark. Thus, if you have no intention of expanding your business beyond state lines and do not have an online presence, registering your trademark at the state level may be the best way to protect your local brand.

In addition, state registration creates a record of the date you began using your trademark. This record may be helpful if you are accused of trademark infringement or if you want to stop another company from using a mark similar to the mark you are using in the same state. Notably, state trademark registration only protects the trademark in the state where it is registered. Therefore, if you are doing business nationally—that is, in more than one state or across state lines—or selling online, procuring a state registration alone (without securing a federally registered mark), is likely not the most prudent approach to protect your brand.

Further, state trademark registration does not give the trademark owner the right to use the ® symbol; however, the trademark owner may use a TM or SM symbol to designate that the mark is being used as a trademark or service mark (explained in chapter four), respectively.

FEDERAL TRADEMARK REGISTRATION

In my experience, most companies cringe at the thought of a competing business using their same or similar brand names, logos, or slogans anywhere in the United States. Thus, obtaining a federal trademark registration is usually the preferred and most beneficial approach, considering the extensive rights and protections that come with it.

A federal trademark registration is obtained through the USPTO. The registration is not automatic upon the filing of a trademark application. The federal trademark registration process is discussed in chapter eight. If you obtain a federal registration for your trademark, you have the exclusive right to use the trademark in all 50 states and U.S. territories for the goods or services sold under the mark. Federal registration also provides notice to the world of your trademark rights, as it will come up in trademark searches of the USPTO records (see chapter one for a discussion on the benefits of federal trademark registration).

Further, federal registration on the "Principal Register" provides a legal presumption that you own the trademark and have the right to use it (see discussion below on the differences between the Principal Register and the Supplemental Register). This eliminates the need to gather evidence to prove your ownership rights in a court of law because you are the presumed owner of the mark. This presumption would have to be rebutted by someone bringing a lawsuit—in other words, the person or entity bringing the lawsuit would have to prove that you are not the owner (see chapter 11 for insights on cancellation proceedings).

Federal registration in the United States also gives you protection nationwide, but it does not protect your trademark in other countries. To protect your trademark in other locations, you need to seek trademark protection in the specific countries where you wish to protect your trademark. Notably, if you seek trademark registration protection in countries that are contracting parties to the Paris Convention, you may claim the filing date of your U.S. trademark application if the foreign application is filed within six months of the date you filed the trademark application with the USPTO.[54] Similarly, if a trademark applicant files for trademark protection in a foreign country and then files a trademark application with the USPTO within six months, the applicant may be able to obtain a priority right within the United States dating back to the original filing date of the trademark application in the foreign jurisdiction.

PRINCIPAL REGISTER VERSUS SUPPLEMENTAL REGISTER

When a trademark application is approved for registration, it is either approved for registration on the Principal Register or the Supplemental Register. The Principal Register is the registry reserved for the most unique trademarks registered (see chapter six for information on what makes a trademark unique). These trademarks are considered "distinctive," meaning the marks are arbitrary, fanciful, or suggestive marks. By contrast, the Supplemental Register is the registry used for nondistinctive marks—that is, trademarks that have not yet acquired distinctiveness or "secondary meaning" (discussed below and in chapter six). When you have a trademark registered on the USPTO's Principal Register, you have implicit proof that your trademark is valid, protected, and enforceable. Additionally, registration on the Principal Register for a trademark related to goods provides the trademark owner with the right to request U.S. Customs and Border Control to stop the importation of infringing goods. In chapter six, I provide more information on how you can increase your chances of having your trademark registered on the Principal Register.

While it is ideal to have your mark registered on the Principal Register, there are still benefits to having a mark registered on the Supplemental Register. Like with the Principal Register, the USPTO will reject and deny the registration of another trademark that is the same or similar to yours if your trademark is listed on the Supplemental Register. Also, you still have the right to use the ® symbol. Additionally, being on the Supplemental Register for five years may be used to prove exclusive use of a mark during that period of time. This is one of the requirements to show acquired distinctiveness for registration on the Principal Register (which would require the filing of a new trademark application after the five-year period).

However, unlike the Principal Register, a mark registered on the Supplemental Register does not have the presumption of federal ownership. This means that if you file a lawsuit or a lawsuit is filed against you, you will need to prove that the relevant public knows of your company, knows of your product or service, and associates the trademark with your product or service. Generally, it is more difficult and costly to prevail in a trademark lawsuit if you are registered on the Supplemental Register.

Notably, if you do not have a registered trademark on either the Principal Register or Supplemental Register and merely have common law trademark rights, you will have the burden of proving you hold "superior" trademark rights to a party accused of infringing your company's trademark rights. In addition, you will not be able to get statutory damages and will be required to prove actual damages that resulted from the infringement. Proving actual damages, in general, is a more difficult and costly endeavor because you need to prove how your business has been negatively impacted and financially harmed as a direct result of the alleged infringement.

IDENTIFYING TRADEMARK APPLICATIONS

When a trademark application is filed, it is given a unique serial number to identify it. Only after a trademark is approved for registration does the USPTO assign the mark a registration number. The following trademark examples are provided for illustrative and educational purposes only and reflect information available in the public records of the USPTO. Neither I nor my law firm represent the companies identified, except for the marks that my law firm owns. Note that the descriptions of services or goods associated with the referenced marks are not necessarily inclusive of all goods or services associated with the mark. As discussed in chapter seven, there are numerous classes of goods and services in which a mark may be filed.

WORD TRADEMARKS

A word mark is a broad type of trademark, as it protects standard characters without regard to style, font, size, or color. Below are examples of federally registered word marks:

WORD TRADEMARK	DESCRIPTION OF GOODS OR SERVICES
AMAZON PRIME	"Customer loyalty program services featuring rewards in the form of discounted shipping services; retail services, namely, administration of a discount program for enabling participants to obtain discounts on shipping services through use of a discount membership program."[55] *U.S. Registration No. 3419886*
Google	"application service provider (ASP) services, namely, hosting computer software applications of others; computer services, namely, providing search engines to allow users to find blogs on a wide variety of topics; computer services, namely, providing a search engine to allow users to search full texts of books, find reviews and other information on books, search for magazine content, and find references books on other wide sites; provision of customized search engines for others; providing technical information in the field of computer software development; providing a web site featuring software development tools and API's (application program interface) for developers."[56] *U.S. Registration No. 4058966*

TRADEMARK GENIE	"Legal services, namely, trademark searching and clearance services, trademark maintenance services, preparation of applications for trademark registration, trademark licensing and litigation of trademarks; providing a website featuring information about intellectual property services relating to search, registration, prosecution, maintenance and monitoring of trademarks."[57] *U.S. Registration No. 6228449* *(filed and owned by my law firm)*
IP GENIE	"Intellectual property legal services."[58] *U.S. Registration No. 6719584* *(filed and owned by my law firm)*

DESIGN/LOGO TRADEMARKS

A design mark, often referred to as a logo mark, protects the design in the form submitted to the USPTO as part of the trademark application. The following are examples of design marks that demonstrate the power of branding using a strong mark (see chapter six for insights into what makes a strong mark):

DESIGN/LOGO TRADEMARK	DESCRIPTION OF GOODS OR SERVICES
amazon	"Providing a searchable on-line database featuring screenplays, music, movies, television shows, comic books, and publications."[59] *U.S. Registration No. 5508999*
(Apple logo)	"Computers [and computer programs recorded on paper and tape]."[60] *U.S. Registration No. 1114431*

Coca-Cola	"Beverages and syrups for the manufacture of such beverages."[61] *U.S. Registration No. 0238146*
M	"Franchise services namely, offering technical assistance in the establishment and/or operations of restaurants."[62] *U.S. Registration No. 1592293*
✓	"Footwear."[63] *U.S. Registration No. 1323343*
STARBUCKS COFFEE	"Coffee [; tea; cocoa; prepared coffee and coffee-based beverages; prepared espresso and espresso-based beverages; beverages made of tea; powdered chocolate and vanilla; flavoring syrups to add to beverages; baked goods, namely, muffins, scones, biscuits, cookies, pastries and breads; sandwiches; hot and cold ready-to-eat fruit and whole grain based breakfast cereal; iced tea, ready-to-drink tea; chocolate food beverages not being dairy-based or vegetable based; ((chocolate food beverages not being dairy-based or vegetable based with coffee flavors;)) cocoa products, namely, cocoa mixes and cocoa powder; hot chocolate; ((cocoa beverages with milk;)) prepared cocoa and cocoa-based beverages; preparations for making chocolate or cocoa-based drinks, namely, liquid and powdered hot chocolate mix and liquid and powdered hot cocoa mix; chocolate and candy, namely, chocolates, chocolate bars, chocolate-covered coffee beans, chocolate truffles, chocolate-covered fruits, chocolate-covered nuts, chocolate-covered dried fruits, chocolate-covered crackers and chocolate toppings]."[64] *U.S. Registration No. 3298945*

P PERKINS LAW BRAND PROTECTION	"Legal services; Providing information about legal services via a website."[65] *U.S. Registration No. 7292180* *(filed and owned by my law firm)*
	"Legal services, namely, trademark searching and clearance services, trademark maintenance services, preparation and filing of applications for trademark registration, trademark licensing and litigation of trademarks; intellectual property legal services; providing a website featuring information about intellectual property legal services relating to search, registration, prosecution, maintenance and monitoring of trademarks; Providing legal guidance on protecting intellectual property assets."[66] *U.S. Registration No. 7304598* *(filed and owned by my law firm)*

SLOGAN TRADEMARKS

The following are examples of trademarks obtained for slogans:

SLOGAN TRADEMARK	DESCRIPTION OF GOODS OR SERVICES
JUST DO IT	"Retail store services and on-line retail store services featuring apparel, apparel accessories, footwear, footwear accessories, headwear, eyewear and accessories, sporting goods and equipment, bags, sports bags, sports and fitness products and accessories."[67] *U.S. Registration No. 5727940*
GET YOUR BRAND ARMOR ON!	"Legal services; Providing information about legal services via a website." *U.S. Registration No. 7333444* *(filed and owned by my law firm)*

If you come up with a catchy and unique slogan, it may be something you are able to secure national rights to by filing a federal trademark registration.

NONTRADITIONAL TRADEMARKS

Essentially, anything that functions as a source identifier may be eligible for registration with the USPTO. In addition to traditional trademarks, there are also nontraditional trademarks. Nontraditional trademarks include the following types of marks: sound, color, scent or smell, motion, hologram, and configuration or shape.

Sound Trademarks

Once I share with you a few examples of sound trademarks, I suspect you will immediately recognize them. The first example is the roar of the lion seen at the beginning of Metro-Goldwyn-Mayer films (U.S. Registration No. 1395550). The second example is the 20th Century Fox sound trademark that accompanies the Hollywood-style spotlights seen at the beginning of the corporation's films (U.S. Registration No. 74629287).

Color Trademarks

Examples of color trademarks are Tiffany blue (U.S. Registration No. 2359351) and the pink of Crumbl cookie boxes (U.S. Registration No. 6305598).

Shape Trademarks

Examples of shape trademarks are the Coca-Cola bottle (U.S. Registration No. 0696147) and the teardrop shape of Hershey's Kisses (U.S. Registration No. 1986822).

Scent/Smell Trademarks

To trademark a scent or smell, the scent must not merely serve a utilitarian purpose such as the scent of a perfume or an air freshener. These types of scents are deemed functional and not registrable. A perfume is deemed functional because it is designed to make you smell attractive and fragrant. Air fresheners are also deemed to be functional because they are designed to make the spaces where they are used smell pleasant. An example of a registered scent is the flowery musk scent in Verizon stores (U.S. Registration No. 4618936). However, based upon a review of the USPTO records, it appears this registration was canceled because the trademark maintenance documents were not filed. I discuss the trademark maintenance filing requirements in chapter ten.

Flip Flop Shops received a scent trademark for the coconut aroma used in their retail locations (U.S. Registration No. 4113191). Based upon a review of the USPTO records, it appears that Flip Flop Shops' scent trademark was also canceled for not filing trademark maintenance documents. Whether or not failing to file the maintenance documents was intentional is unknown.

As discussed in chapter ten, it is common that the required maintenance documents are not filed. Common reasons maintenance documents are not timely filed are the deadline not being calendared and tracked or the email address with the USPTO not being kept current, resulting in the courtesy reminder emails not being received. Other reasons why a company may not file maintenance documents are if it is no longer using the mark as registered (in other words, it revised or modified its trademark) or discontinuing use of the registered mark in commerce.

Motion and Hologram Trademarks

As a result of digital technology, there are innovative ways to advertise and market a company's brand. As such, it is becoming more popular for brand owners to use technology to create and protect new forms of trademarks, such as motion and hologram. An example of a motion trademark is that which appears when Microsoft Windows is started (U.S. Registration No. 3926321). The motion is described as follows: "The mark consists of an animated sequence that begins with four objects of colored light (one each in the color red, green, yellow and blue) that appear in a staggered sequence and swirl around one another in distinct arcs, expanding in size and illumination intensity until they converge and form a four paneled flag image with a circular white light in the center that oscillates with varying illumination intensity. The Color Black represents background and is not part of the mark."[68]

However, based upon a review of the USPTO records, the referenced Microsoft Windows motion trademark was canceled for not filing the required maintenance documents.

Another example of a motion trademark is the opening of the Lamborghini wing door (U.S. Registration No. 2793439). The description of the mark states in part that "The mark consists of the unique motion in which the door of a vehicle is opened. The doors move parallel to the body of the vehicle but are gradually raised above the vehicle to a parallel position."[69]

Hologram trademark registration is challenging to obtain from the USPTO because, in general, a hologram standing alone does not function as an exclusively unique source identifier, as they are commonly used on various similar products. The Trademark Trial and Appeal Board states that "the common use of holograms for non-trademark purposes means that consumers would be less likely to perceive applicant's uses of holograms as trademarks."[70]

An example of a hologram trademark is the mark found on the surface of some American Express credit cards (U.S. Registration No. 3045251).

NONREGISTRABLE TRADEMARKS

There are certain types of marks that cannot receive federal registration in the United States. For instance, if a mark is found in any way to be deceptive, scandalous, disparaging, or contain the name of a living U.S. President, it cannot be registered with the USPTO.[71] An example of a deceptive trademark would be the use of the word "Washington" to describe apples that are not harvested from the State of Washington.

THE METAVERSE

An emerging area of trademark law is the protection of trademarks for digital assets in the metaverse. These assets primarily exist in cyberspace—a virtual, fantasy world where users can interact with each other from the comfort of their own homes. If your company intends to sell branded goods or services in the metaverse, it is advisable to file a trademark application as soon as possible in the relevant international classification of goods and services and jurisdictions so that your mark is protected in the metaverse.

BEWARE OF SCAMS

There are companies that send out misleading notices and offers that appear to be things you need to pay to ensure your trademarks are protected. It is important to note that the USPTO will never send these types of solicitations, nor will the USPTO ever ask you to provide your social security number or credit card payment information over the phone or by email. So, always use caution, let common sense be your guide, and be on the lookout for impostors and fraudsters claiming to be from the USPTO.

Further, if you are considering using a nonattorney trademark service company, also be aware that, generally, nonattorney registration service providers are not the same as using a licensed attorney. In fact, many nonattorney companies have gotten themselves into hot water and been flagged or disciplined by the USPTO for engaging in misleading or illicit solicitation. If you receive a suspicious letter or email, I encourage you to first confirm that the correspondence is coming from a legitimate and credible source. The USPTO's legitimate email addresses will end in "@USPTO. gov." Also, note that the USPTO's offices are currently located in Alexandria, Virginia, so if you receive correspondence referencing a different city, view this as a red flag.

The USPTO consistently provides updates on known scams on its website www.uspto.gov.[72] You can check the site to see if the company from which you received communication is listed by the USPTO as an entity that has been identified or disciplined for sending misleading notices to applicants and registrants. The USPTO site also shows examples of scam notices and provides contact information to report a misleading or scam notice. My law firm received a misleading scam letter related to its registered mark "Trademark Genie." I have included a copy of this sample scam letter at the back of the book.

Fortunately, courts are cracking down on fraudulent behavior. In 2020, a non-U.S. citizen defendant in South Carolina was arrested and charged with crimes related to two trademark renewal solicitation scams involving entities named "Patent and

Trademark Office" and "Patent and Trademark Bureau." During the case, evidence revealed that the defendant had created a false impression to suggest the above-referenced entities were associated with the official United States Patent and Trademark Office. The evidence also showed that the defendant had engaged in a scheme to misrepresent and cause trademark registrants to believe that their registrations were going to expire earlier than they actually were. The fees charged for renewing registrations were higher than those actually charged by the USPTO. The evidence also showed that the defendant had not (and legally could not) renew the registrations.

Although the defendant ended up pleading guilty to four counts of mail fraud as part of a plea agreement, the ultimate penalty was very severe. The federal court sentenced the defendant to more than four years in federal prison and required payment of over $4.5 million in restitution.[73]

What I hope you have learned by now is that the selection of your company's brand—its trademark—is important for the success of your business in terms of distinguishing it from others and staying out of hot water by avoiding unknowingly infringing on someone else's rights.

Congratulations on your commitment to learning why brand protection matters and taking the time to read this book to educate yourself on these important topics. Knowledge is power. So, stay tuned. I will discuss what makes a mark trademarkable in the next chapter!

CHAPTER 6

What Makes a Brand Name Trademarkable?

IN THIS CHAPTER, I DISCUSS WHAT MAKES A WORD, DESIGN MARK, or logo trademarkable. If you are interested in being able to protect your brand in all the United States and its territories, the goal is to select a trademark that is federally registrable and legally protectable. By doing so, you increase your chances of being able to register your mark with the USPTO. Once you have obtained a federal trademark registration, you will be able to enforce your rights against competitors who are using the same or similar mark to the one you have registered.

OBSTACLES TO OBTAINING FEDERAL REGISTRATION

Likelihood of confusion and descriptiveness are common grounds the USPTO cites when refusing to register a trademark or service mark. The rationale in refusing to register a mark deemed to be too similar to another trademark is to avoid confusing consumers about the source of the goods or services. For example, if a woman named Wendy wanted to name her hamburger restaurant after herself and she attempted to register her mark with the USPTO, the USPTO would likely reject her application because consumers may become confused about the source of the goods or services. That is, customers would wonder whether the goods or services "Wendy" wants to sell are in any way associated with the famous "Wendy's" fast-food chain (U.S. Registration No. 4460097).

YOUR TRADEMARK CANNOT CREATE A LIKELIHOOD OF CONFUSION

The test to determine whether there is a likelihood of confusion focuses on two primary questions: (1) are the trademarks confusingly similar and (2) are the goods or services related? Marks are similar if they look alike, sound alike, have similar meanings, or create a similar commercial impression. Goods and services are related if consumers mistakenly believe the goods and services come from the same source. If you are scratching your head wondering how you will determine this, no worries. A trademark attorney will be able to guide you.

By now, you may be thinking of a company that uses the same brand name as another company and wondering how that can be allowed given the information I have shared with you. The reason is that identical trademarks may coexist if the goods or services are not related. For example, the trademark Dove is owned by Unilever, which uses this mark as a brand name for soap. By comparison, the trademark Dove, owned by Mars Inc., is used as a brand name for ice cream and chocolate. Even though the two brand names are spelled and pronounced the same way, these two trademarks are permitted to coexist because the identical brand names are used by companies to market and sell goods or services in completely different and unrelated consumer markets. This, however, is not always the case.

It is important to note that just because a mark is being used for different goods or services does not automatically mean there can never be any likelihood of confusion. The likelihood of confusion analysis is based on many factors, including the strength of the owner's mark, similarity of the marks, proximity of the goods and services, similarity of the trade channels, evidence of actual confusion, defendant's intent, likelihood of expansion, and consumer sophistication. The likelihood of confusion analysis comes down to reviewing and analyzing the detailed facts and circumstances for each particular situation. If you are in a position where a competitor asserts a likelihood of confusion argument against you and demands that you stop using a mark, or conversely, you want to assert such an argument against another entity to prevent the illicit use of your own mark, I urge you to retain an attorney who is experienced in addressing this type of issue. Because these types of matters can quickly become complicated, and perhaps even backfire if you think you have the upper hand and it turns out you do not, it is not advisable to try to tackle such matters on your own.

YOUR TRADEMARK MUST BE DISTINCTIVE

A mark can only become trademarkable through the federal register if it is considered "distinctive." Distinctiveness is often determined by whether the trademark helps to distinguish one brand's products or services from a competitor's products or services. However, distinctiveness is not a cut-and-dried standard. The USPTO assesses and ranks potential trademarks based on their strength as marks to determine whether they are entitled to federal trademark protection. The strength of a trademark determines what level of protection it is entitled to receive in the United States. Trademarks are generally categorized into the following levels of strength, ranging from weak to strong:

- Generic
- Descriptive
- Suggestive
- Arbitrary
- Fanciful

Weak trademarks are not generally entitled to protection. The following image depicts the relative strength of a trademark:

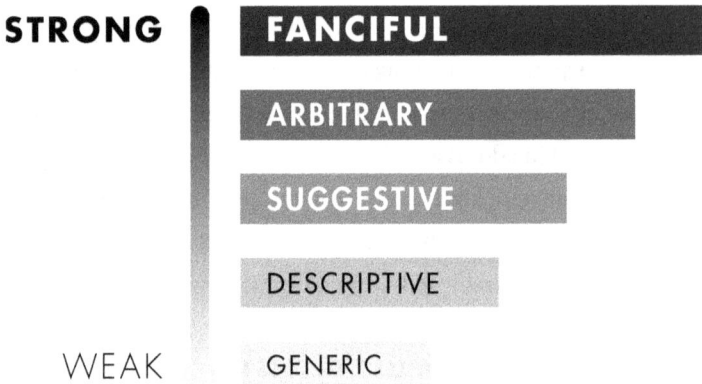

STRONG

FANCIFUL

ARBITRARY

SUGGESTIVE

DESCRIPTIVE

WEAK   GENERIC

The stronger the mark, the more likely it will become registered with the USPTO and entitled to national protection. By comparison, weak trademarks are problematic because they are not entitled to the same legal protections as strong trademarks, and they are difficult and costly to defend.

GENERIC MARKS WILL NOT OBTAIN A FEDERAL REGISTRATION

Generic marks are common, everyday words or phrases that describe a good or service. Generic terms cannot be protected as trademarks because they do not distinguish a particular source or origin of the goods or services. For example, the term *apple* cannot be registered as a trademark associated with selling apples.

Allowing a business to trademark a generic term would essentially give that business a monopoly and would unfairly restrict competitors from effectively describing their products. For this reason, generic marks, which many companies choose to use (perhaps because they do not know any better), may never be registered as trademarks and are therefore the weakest type of mark.

DESCRIPTIVE MARKS ARE WEAK MARKS AND HAVE LIMITATIONS

A mark that simply describes a product or service is considered a descriptive mark. When a trademark merely describes something about the good or service, such as "an ingredient, quality, characteristic, function, feature, purpose, or use of the specified goods or services," it will be considered descriptive.[74] A great example is "Hot and Fresh" for selling coffee or "Swiss" for selling cheese. These words and phrases simply describe the product and, therefore, cannot be trademarked.

A descriptive mark is inherently weak and cannot be registered on the USPTO's Principal Register (recall the discussion in chapter five on the Principal Register versus the Supplemental Register). The exception to this rule is when an applicant can show the mark has acquired distinctiveness or secondary meaning. However, descriptive trademarks may be registered on the Supplemental Register. Further, after five years of consistent use of the mark, a descriptive mark may be able to qualify for registration on the Principal Register. Going from the Supplemental Register to the Principal Register requires an applicant to file a new trademark application. Ultimately, it is generally better for a company to create a strong brand name from the beginning so that the mark can qualify to be placed on the Principal Register.

TRADEMARKS THAT ACQUIRE DISTINCTIVENESS OR SECONDARY MEANING CAN BE REGISTERED

Establishing that a mark has acquired distinctiveness or secondary meaning involves an analysis of the facts and circumstances of the particular situation. A mark is deemed to have acquired distinctiveness or secondary meaning when the mark has been in use long enough or garnered enough consumer recognition in the marketplace that when consumers see the mark, they primarily relate it to a specific company (or source) as opposed to merely relating it to the particular services or products the mark describes.

By acquiring distinctiveness or secondary meaning, a mark is allowed to be registered and enforced even if it is descriptive. The type of evidence that may be used to establish acquired distinctiveness or secondary meaning includes consumer surveys; sales and advertising figures; length of use; media coverage; and testimony from industry experts, customers, or other people who can attest to the mark's association with the owner's goods or services. The type and amount of evidence required to establish distinctiveness varies depending on the circumstances and the jurisdiction in which the matter is pending.

SUGGESTIVE MARKS ARE GENERALLY STRONG MARKS AND CAN BE REGISTERED

A suggestive mark suggests or hints at something about the goods or services without explicitly stating it. It creates a connection in one's mind about the type of product the mark represents. The biggest difference between a descriptive mark and a suggestive mark is that a consumer will need to use thought and imagination to understand the suggestive mark's connection to the product. Depending on the mark's uniqueness, a suggestive mark is considered strong to very strong and is generally protectable. The mark Coppertone for suntan lotion (U.S. Registration No. 09178250) is an example because it implies or suggests someone who uses the lotion will get a copper-colored tan. Another example of a suggestive trademark is Jaguar for cars (U.S. Registration No. 5506095), as it suggests the car is very fast and associates the car's elegant design and speed with that of the elegance and strength of the animal.

Suggestive marks offer more protection than either descriptive or generic marks; however, suggestive marks can also come under scrutiny. In short, it is not always easy to tell whether a mark is suggestive or descriptive, and it may become expensive and time-consuming to analyze the marks to try to make this argument.

ARBITRARY AND FANCIFUL TRADEMARKS ARE THE STRONGEST TYPES OF MARKS

Arbitrary and fanciful trademarks are the strongest type of mark and the most likely to become registered. An arbitrary trademark is a type of mark that consists of common terms or known phrases but does not describe or suggest anything about the product or service. In other words, arbitrary marks are actual words that have no association with the goods or services to which the words relate.

A well-known example of an arbitrary mark is Apple for computers (U.S. Registration No. 1078312). While *apple* is a real word—a type of fruit—it is an arbitrary use of the word because there is no inherent connection between the fruit and the computer. Another example of an arbitrary mark is Camel for cigarettes (U.S. Registration No. 0126760). Again, there is no inherent connection between cigarettes and the humpbacked desert animal. In other words, an arbitrary trademark is essentially taking a familiar, common word and giving it a new meaning by associating it with different products or services.

Fanciful marks are invented words with no meaning in any language. They are invented for the purpose of being a trademark for the product or service. Fanciful marks are registrable with the USPTO. A popular example is Häagen-Dazs, which is a word made up by the producer of the ice cream brand (U.S. Registration No. 0737244). Although the term alludes to a Danish origin, the word is not Danish and means nothing in any language. Other examples of fanciful marks include Xerox for photocopiers (U.S. Registration No. 79074696) and Kodak for photographic film (U.S. Registration No. 0399092). These marks are made-up words, and because the words have no association with copiers or film, they are deemed very strong, fanciful trademarks. They have no meaning outside their use as trademark-identifying sources, and therefore, they do not restrict competition if they receive federal trademark protection. Ideally, it is best and safest to create and use a fanciful mark.

As you can see, the relative strength and distinctiveness of a trademark are important and may determine whether the trademark is registrable or not with the USPTO. Not every trademark is registrable, and there is no guarantee you will obtain federal registration merely by filing a trademark application with the USPTO. Therefore, taking the time to create an arbitrary or fanciful mark is the best practice to ensure the strength of a mark. However, that said, there may be circumstances in which it may be best for a business to create a more descriptive or suggestive mark. For instance, when the company wants to have its brand name more directly and clearly reflect the types of services or goods the business provides.

One of the things I very much enjoy doing with my clients is guiding them and helping them brainstorm brand names that are distinctive so they can create a strong and protectable brand name. To do this, I first work with my clients to explore various potential brand names they have thought of or like for their business. I then conduct trademark searches to determine whether any other entity is using the same or a similar name or mark in the marketplace. If so, then I work with the client to determine whether the name or mark is being used to advertise or sell related goods or services or if there is another reason to not pursue using a particular name. I will discuss the trademark search process in the next chapter.

CHAPTER 7

Search Before You Leap

IF YOU ARE ALREADY IN BUSINESS OPERATING UNDER A CERTAIN brand name or multiple brand names, you may be wondering whether you will be able to obtain federal trademark registration or if you are using a brand name that infringes on another company's rights. Or, if you are in the process of setting up your business and creating a brand name or new product name, you may be wondering how to figure out whether the brand name you have chosen is entitled to federal trademark protection. Regardless of whether you are currently in business or just starting a new business or product line, the process used to determine and analyze where you stand is similar.

First, it is definitely most prudent to conduct a trademark search to make sure the coast is clear, so to speak, before you leap into using a brand name in your business endeavors. A search is necessary to check whether a mark is already being used by another entity. As I have discussed in previous chapters, if you do not take the time to conduct a proper trademark search, you may find yourself embroiled in a legal dispute that could have been avoided. Remember, even if no one has yet challenged your use of a brand, if you later learn that you are using someone else's mark, you may be infringing on their trademark rights. As such, it is better to know this information sooner versus later so you have time to consider all your options, including whether or not you will perhaps need to rebrand your business. Rebranding your business with a plan in mind for how to do so is much wiser than becoming entangled in a situation where you are required to reinvent the proverbial wheel and rebrand when you are under the gun to do so.

Second, it is important to know that there are different types of searches that can be conducted to help you learn whether your brand name is already being used and whether or not it is prudent for you to proceed with using particular words or designs to represent your brand. The process of searching for conflicting trademarks before either using a mark or applying for federal trademark registration is referred to as a "clearance search." A clearance search involves checking to see if a particular trademark is already being used or has already been registered at the USPTO by someone else.

CLEARANCE SEARCH

Before you start conducting a clearance search, the first step is to identify the particular words and designs you wish to use to represent your brand, as these will be the elements that form the basis of your clearance search. I am a strong advocate of engaging an experienced brand protection attorney to assist you with conducting a clearance search, principally because search results can easily be misinterpreted. That said, if you want to tackle a preliminary search on your own, I have included a link to resources in the Additional Information section at the back of the book where you can download a proprietary worksheet to help you stay organized. Even if you do decide to engage an attorney (which is a smart decision), compiling the information that is suggested in the worksheet will assist you in your conversations with legal counsel, which may also save you time and money.

Once you have identified the words and designs you wish to

search, I recommend that you next identify the type of goods or services you plan to associate with the mark. For example, clothing, electronics, food, entertainment services, professional services, et cetera are all product markets within which companies engage in business. You will need to associate your business with a market because assigning a business "classification" is the next step in conducting a search. Knowing your business classification will also be required when you move forward in submitting a trademark application with the USPTO. The USPTO breaks down goods and services into classifications to help with this.

CLASSES OF GOODS AND SERVICES

In the United States, trademarks are grouped into 45 different classes (referred to as international classes), or categories, that cover all goods and services. Within the 45 general categories, 35 relate to different classes of goods (i.e., classes 1–34) and ten relate to different classes of services (i.e., classes 35–45).[75] The following list shows what each class generally covers:[76]

Goods

001 Chemicals

002 Paints

003 Cosmetics and cleaning preparations

004 Lubricants and fuels

005 Pharmaceuticals

006 Metal goods

007 Machinery

008 Hand tools

009 Electrical and scientific apparatuses

010 Medical apparatuses

011 Environmental control apparatuses

012 Vehicles

013 Firearms

014 Jewelry

015 Musical instruments

016 Paper goods and printed matter

017 Rubber goods

018 Leather goods

019 Nonmetallic building materials

020 Furniture and articles not otherwise classified

021 Housewares and glass

022 Cordage and fibers

023 Yarns and threads

024 Fabrics

025 Clothing

026 Fancy goods

027 Floor coverings

028 Toys and sporting goods

029 Meats and processed foods

030 Staple foods

031 Natural agricultural products

032 Light beverages

033 Wines and spirits

034 Smokers' articles

Services

035 Advertising and business

036 Insurance and financial

037 Building construction and repair

038 Telecommunication

039 Transportation and storage

040 Treatment of materials

041 Education and entertainment

042 Computer and scientific

043 Hotels and restaurants

044 Medical, beauty, and agricultural

045 Personal and legal

The USPTO website and the USPTO's Trademark ID Manual both provide more detailed information on what each class covers, and both are very helpful to reference when determining the appropriate class or classes that cover your company's goods or services.[77]

It is not uncommon for a trademark to be filed in numerous classes to ensure the mark receives the most comprehensive trademark protection. Notably, this does not mean that separate trademark applications must be filed since a trademark owner may select multiple classes within the same application. However, under some circumstances, more than one trademark application may be necessary to protect a company's brand.

TRADEMARK APPLICATION FILINGS VERSUS TRADEMARK REGISTRATIONS

Numerous trademark applications are filed with the USPTO every year. The following chart depicts the number of trademark application filings (based on the number of classes) submitted between 2020 and 2022:[78]

YEAR	NUMBER OF TRADEMARK APPLICATION FILINGS BASED ON NUMBER OF CLASSES
2020	738,112
2021	943,928
2022	787,795

By contrast, the number of new trademark registrations by fiscal year based on the total classes registered in 2020 through 2022 is depicted in the following graph:[79]

YEAR	NUMBER OF TRADEMARK APPLICATION FILINGS BASED ON NUMBER OF CLASSES
2020	400,298
2021	434,810
2022	453,588

TRADEMARK "KNOCKOUT" SEARCHES

A trademark knockout search is a type of trademark search that is conducted using records found within the United States Patent and Trademark Office's database, which is called the Trademark Electronic Search System, or TESS for short. At minimum, this type of search should be conducted before submitting a trademark application to the USPTO.

See the Additional Information section at the back of this book for the link to conduct a search of the USPTO database. Essentially, searching the TESS database will reveal whether there are any active trademarks similar to the trademark you are using or thinking of using. Note that there may be a delay in the database's records because it takes time for new trademark application filings to appear, and therefore, it is possible that a recently filed trademark will not be discovered with a TESS search.

I highly recommend that you have an attorney review and analyze the information and findings of your searches so you do not unintentionally step onto a land mine. Competently interpreting the results of a trademark search takes skill and knowledge, so it makes sense to engage a trademark attorney to assist with the analysis and guide you accordingly.

If a trademark search reveals that a mark is being used for goods or services that are unlike the goods or services your business provides, or appears to be different from the terms or words you intend to use with your brand, I again recommend that you speak with an attorney versed in trademarks before you conclude that you have a green light to continue to use or begin using the mark and possibly file a trademark application with the USPTO. If you happen to get a bad hit—meaning that the results of the search show that another company is using the same or a similar trademark for the same or similar types of goods or services—it is usually best to consider pivoting and begin exploring other trademark options.

LIVE VERSUS DEAD MARKS

The records obtained through a USPTO search will reflect whether the registrations of similar marks are "live" or "dead." A live trademark registration means the trademark is being maintained and continues to exist as a registered mark, whereas a dead trademark registration indicates that it is no longer active. A trademark might be flagged as inactive or dead if, for instance, the trademark lapsed because the trademark owner failed to timely file the required maintenance documents with the USPTO or the trademark was canceled for other reasons (for example, the mark was no longer being used or the mark was challenged and the registration was revoked). Moreover, even if a trademark appears in the USPTO database as a dead mark, this does not mean the coast is automatically clear for you to move forward with using the mark.

As I have addressed in previous chapters, and will address in the chapters that follow, a mark may be listed as dead and canceled if the trademark owner fails to file the necessary maintenance documents even if the trademark owner continues to use the trademark. If this is the scenario, your trademark attorney will be able to guide you and flesh out whether it makes business sense to proceed with filing a trademark application for the mark or continue to use the mark, understanding that the owner of the dead mark who lost their federal trademark rights may still have common law rights for the dead mark. Generally, it is always best to have federal trademark rights over common law rights if possible. Refer to the discussion in chapter one regarding the benefits of federal trademark registration and the discussion in chapter five regarding common law trademark rights if you wish to review the reasons for this.

The USPTO uses only live registrations as a basis for refusal or rejection. Thus, it is important to determine whether a party with a dead mark in the USPTO database is still using the trademark and can claim common law rights. Remember, a company with common law rights may still be able to preclude you from obtaining federal trademark rights. Also, recall that even if you are successful in obtaining federal trademark rights, you will not be able to stop a company that acquired common law trademark rights before you from using your mark.

Unfortunately, it happens all too often that trademark owners miss trademark maintenance deadlines, which results in the USPTO canceling the mark and labeling the mark as dead in the USPTO database (see chapter 11 for a discussion on trademark cancellation proceedings).

FIRST USE OF A TRADEMARK PREVAILS

Just because you obtain a federal registration does not mean you have the right to stop another party from using the same mark if they started using the same or a similar mark in their business before you did. I once received a call from an attorney who contacted me for my opinion and guidance on a situation related to a trademark he had federally registered with the USPTO. The attorney did not practice intellectual property law. He had obtained a trademark registration for a mark he was using and discovered that another lawyer was using the same trademark. Unfortunately, he was not able to stop the other attorney from using the mark because the other attorney's use predated his own.

This is a situation that could have been avoided if he had done a comprehensive trademark search to find out whether anyone else was using the same mark before he started using the mark and spent the effort and money to obtain a federal trademark registration. Sadly, he was faced with the situation of deciding whether he should rebrand his business to avoid having potential clients confuse his services with those of the other attorney.

COMPREHENSIVE TRADEMARK SEARCH

While it is possible to search various databases and social media accounts one by one, the best way to determine whether there are any entities with common law rights related to the trademark you seek to use or protect is to engage an attorney to conduct a comprehensive search, analyze the information obtained, and provide an opinion addressing the relative risk in proceeding with using or registering the mark. Again, knowledge is power. The more information you have, the better prepared you will be to navigate the land mines and take an appropriate course of action given the facts and circumstances of the particular situation.

A comprehensive trademark search can be expanded to countries outside of the United States as well if you are considering doing business in another jurisdiction. Depending on what your business plans are regarding the jurisdictions in which you sell or plan to sell your goods or services, it may also make sense to ensure your search is broad enough to determine whether the proposed mark is being used in other jurisdictions. Even if you do not plan to sell your goods or services in a jurisdiction outside of the United States, it is good to know if there is a company outside of the U.S. that is selling the same or similar goods or services under that same brand name. The reason for this is that most companies today have established an online presence that includes, at the very least, a website and various social media platforms. It could potentially cause confusion for a consumer when searching on the internet and create a negative image for your brand if the other company using the same mark has a bad reputation, for example. This could be a situation where it just makes sense to come up with a different brand name to avoid these issues.

In my experience, comprehensive trademark searches are well worth the investment. I have witnessed countless occasions where the results of a comprehensive search proved to be extremely helpful in guiding next steps for my clients. For example, I helped a client who was setting up a business using a certain brand name and wanted to know whether she could protect the name with a federal trademark. When we conducted the comprehensive search, we determined that proceeding with the desired trademark was high risk because another company (with very deep pockets) was using a similar name. My client decided to take a conservative approach and pivoted sooner versus later to minimize her risk by selecting another brand name. Ultimately, her decision to do so paid off. With my guidance, this client created a very strong brand name using a made-up (fanciful) word and now owns a federally protected trademark with exclusive rights to use that mark across the United States.

When my firm is engaged to conduct a U.S. comprehensive search, in addition to searching the USPTO database, we also search the databases of all U.S. states for registered trademarks. As for the common law search component, a U.S. comprehensive search report includes the results from searching more than 20 million secretary of state business records for both identical and similar results; searching domain names for identical and very similar results from more than 1,600 domain name extensions; a web search combining the trademark name with significant key-words; a web search for images associated with the mark name; searching the largest social media platforms (Facebook, LinkedIn, Twitter, Instagram, and Pinterest); and searching social names, which reveals whether the trademark name is registered as a user name in a vast number of social networks.

DESIGN SEARCH CODES

If your mark includes a design element, you must conduct a search using a design code. A list of design search codes can be found on the USPTO website, the link to which I have included in the Additional Information section located at the back of this book. A design code search may also be done through the USPTO's TESS database.

The USPTO assigns all marks that contain design elements numerical codes, which are used for search purposes by the USPTO. For example, my law firm filed the following logo/design mark for use in association with legal services:

The USPTO assigned the following design search codes (see U.S. Registration Number 7304598):

02.11.07 - Arms; fingers; hands; human hands, fingers, arms

09.05.03 - Fezzes, turbans, berets, other visorless and brimless hats

26.01.27 - Circles containing irregular exterior lining or elements not amounting to a decorative border

26.03.13 - Ovals, exactly two (not concentric); two ovals

26.03.28 - Miscellaneous designs with overall oval shape, including amoeba-like shapes and irregular ovals; oval shape (miscellaneous overall shape)

26.05.21 - Triangles that are completely or partially shaded

26.05.25 - Triangles with one or more curved sides

Deciding what terms and designs to search for and interpreting the results can be complicated. If a company using the same trademark is identified, more research should be done to ascertain who used the mark first, the nature of the use, and the types of goods or services that are associated with the mark. The earlier user, providing the use is sufficient, will always have superior rights in the jurisdiction where the mark is being used. These reports are indeed comprehensive and can often consist of hundreds of pages of information.

I hope the big takeaway for you from this chapter is to always do a comprehensive trademark search so you can maximize your investment and minimize your risk moving forward.

In the next chapter, I will discuss the trademark application process and timeline.

CHAPTER 8

Trademark Application Process and Timeline

IN THIS CHAPTER, I PROVIDE A GENERAL OVERVIEW OF THE trademark application process, explain the application timeline, and outline the information you will need to process a trademark application with the USPTO. As I have discussed in previous chapters, to obtain a registered trademark in the United States, you must start by filing a trademark application with the USPTO.

TRADEMARK HISTORY

Here is some trademark history for you. The first registered U.S. trademark was issued on October 25, 1870, to Averill Chemical Paint Company of New York, depicting an eagle holding a paint brush.[80] The oldest U.S. design trademark for a food product still in use today (depicted below, albeit in a modified form) was registered on November 29, 1870, by the William Underwood Co. of Boston, Massachusetts, for use on canned ham products.[81]

Underwood's design represents one of the first successful canning companies in the United States, and it serves as a source identifier for Underwood's "Deviled Entremets . . . Intended for Sandwiches, Luncheons, and Traveler's Repasts."[82] Honestly, I had to look up the meanings of the words *entremets* and *repasts*. According to the Merriam-Webster dictionary, entremets are "dishes served in addition to the main course of a meal,"[83] and *repasts* means "something taken as food" and "the act or time of taking food."[84]

SPECIFY THE TYPE OF TRADEMARK

By the time you are ready to file a trademark application, you should have already identified the mark you seek to protect and completed a trademark search to determine if it is already in use in the marketplace (see the discussion about conducting trademark searches in chapter seven). The application requires the mark format be identified—that is, whether the mark appears as a standard character mark, a special form mark (meaning a stylized or design mark), or as a sound mark. Each type requires submitting a separate trademark application.

IDENTIFY THE OWNER OF THE TRADEMARK

Correctly identifying the proper owner of the trademark is key to securing trademark rights and maintaining those rights. The trademark application may only be filed by the owner of the trademark, and the applicant is required to identify the name of the owner of the trademark in the trademark application. The owner of the trademark can be an individual, a corporate entity, or a partnership. Sometimes, a trademark is owned by an IP holding company that licenses the use of the trademark. Essentially, the party who controls the nature and quality of the goods or services used in connection with the trademark should be the trademark owner. It is the owner of a trademark who is able to recognize the value of the trademark for accounting purposes, use the mark as a security interest, and determine when to enforce the mark against infringers. Therefore, the correct identification of the owner of the trademark is critical to avoid losing your trademark rights.

INCLUDE A DRAWING OF THE MARK

An applicant must submit a depiction of the trademark, referred to as "a drawing." The drawing must be clear, and it can either be a standard character mark in the form of a word or phrase or a special form mark (also referred to as a stylized mark/logo). Examples of standard character marks which were referenced in chapter five are "Just Do It" and "Trademark Genie." The following examples of special form marks are provided for illustrative and educational purposes only, and reflect information available in the public records of the USPTO. Neither I nor my law firm represent Coca-Cola. The words *Coca-Cola* in the highly recognizable stylized font was registered on January 31, 1893:

(U.S. Registration No. 0022406)

The shape of the Coca-Cola bottle was registered on April 12, 1960:

(U.S. Registration No. 0696147)

And the Coca- Cola logo was registered on June 19, 2007:

(U.S. Registration No. 3252896).

SELECT FILING BASIS

The trademark application requires the applicant to indicate the "filing basis" for the application. There are four general filing bases:

1. **Use in commerce.** This basis is appropriate if the mark is currently being used in commerce in association with your goods or services. This is referred to as a 1(a) or "use-based" trademark application (i.e., under the Trademark Act Section 1(a)).

2. **Intent-to-use.** This basis is appropriate if there is a bona fide intention to use the mark in commerce in association with your goods or services in the near future. This basis is often referred to as a 1(b) (i.e., under the Trademark Act Section 1(b)) or "intent-to-use" (ITU) trademark application.

3. **Foreign registration.** This basis is appropriate if the applicant owns a foreign registration of the same mark for the same goods or services in their country of origin. This basis is under Section 44(e) of the Trademark Act.

4. **Foreign application**. This basis is appropriate if the applicant owns an earlier-filed foreign application for the same mark and goods or services that was filed within the six months preceding filing the U.S. trademark application. This basis is referred to as a "foreign priority basis" because an applicant is requesting a filing date for their U.S. trademark application that is the same date as the foreign application filing date. This basis is under Section 44(d) of the Trademark Act.

This chapter will focus on the use in commerce filing and the intent-to-use filing bases. Filing basis affects the examination process and the requirements for the application. For example, if an application is filed under an intent-to-use basis, the applicant must file a Statement of Use (SOU) before the trademark can be registered. If the application is filed under the use in commerce basis, an appropriate specimen showing the use of the mark in association with the goods or services must be filed at the time the trademark application is filed.

DATES OF FIRST USE

The trademark application requires that the trademark owner specify the date of first use of the mark anywhere and the date of first use of the mark in commerce. The meanings of these terms, in my experience, are often misunderstood. The date of first use anywhere is the date the goods were first sold or transported or the services were first rendered under the mark in the ordinary course of trade. The date of first use in commerce is the date the goods or services were sold or rendered under the mark across state lines in the ordinary course of trade. The date of first use anywhere will either be before or the same as the date of first use in commerce.

REQUESTS FOR EXTENSION OF TIME TO FILE A STATEMENT OF USE

If the applicant is not ready to file an SOU within six months of the mark being issued a notice of allowance, a request for extension of time to file a Statement of Use must be filed to avoid abandonment of the application. Filing a request for an extension of time is a common occurrence. An extension request is a sworn statement whereby the applicant states that they still have a bona fide intention to use the trademark in commerce and require additional time to start using the mark. The request for extension of time also requires additional fees be paid for each class of goods or services. To be approved, each extension request must also be correctly filed (that is, it must satisfy all the filing requirements) before the expiration of a previously granted application. If a punctual extension of time is not filed, the mark will become abandoned, and the USPTO will reflect the mark as dead in TESS.

An applicant may file up to five requests for extensions of time to file a Statement of Use (each of which provides a six-month extension), providing the applicant includes evidence of a good reason why the extension request is necessary. Thus, the applicant may have a maximum of three years from the date the notice of allowance is issued to file the Statement of Use showing that the mark is being used in commerce in association with the goods and services identified in the trademark application. It is not unusual for a trademark owner to file several or all of the allowable extension requests to buy more time to properly use the mark in commerce before filing an SOU with an appropriate specimen or specimens of use.

If an SOU is not filed prior to the expiration of the fifth extension of time, the mark is deemed abandoned, and if the trademark owner still wishes to proceed with obtaining federal trademark protection, a new trademark application will need to be filed. If a new application is filed, the process starts all over again from the beginning.

As a practical matter, if an applicant is close to the deadline to file the Statement of Use, I recommend that a request for extension of time be filed at the same time as the filing of the Statement of Use because the applicant will not know whether the specimen submitted will be accepted and will not want the time to submit an acceptable specimen to expire. By doing so, the applicant will be protected from the mark being abandoned or canceled if the specimen submitted is not deemed acceptable by the USPTO, as there will be more time to submit an acceptable specimen.

BENEFIT TO FILING AN INTENT-TO-USE TRADEMARK APPLICATION

While there are definitely advantages to filing an intent-to-use trademark application versus waiting for a mark to be in use before filing the application, there are additional costs associated with an ITU application compared to an application based upon use in commerce.

A major benefit to filing an ITU trademark application is that the date the application is filed is deemed the constructive date of first use and can be determinative of who will win a trademark battle if another party starts using the same or a confusingly similar trademark after the date you filed an intent-to-use application.

I have personally experienced how an ITU trademark application was worth the investment with regard to the Trademark Genie word mark. Another applicant filed a use in commerce trademark application for the same trademark after my firm filed its ITU trademark application. Although the other filer's use of the mark purportedly predated my firm's ITU trademark application, the USPTO issued a final office action denying the registration of the other mark because my firm's ITU application was filed first.

IDENTIFY CLASSES OF GOODS OR SERVICES

The applicant is required to identify the classes of goods or services under which they seek trademark protection. This is required in addition to providing a description of the goods or services for which they are seeking trademark protection. The scope of the description of the goods or services cannot be expanded within the same application once it is filed, but the scope can be narrowed.

The description of goods or services is very important. As previously mentioned, there are 45 different classes within which a trademark owner may seek to obtain trademark registration. Inaccurate and unacceptable identifications can result in a refusal to register your trademark. For the broadest federal protection, it is prudent to include all the classes that apply.

For example, my firm's Trademark Genie word mark was filed in two classes, but not at the same time. The first application was filed as an ITU application under class 45 for "Legal services, namely, trademark searching and clearance services, trademark maintenance services, preparation of applications for trademark registration, trademark licensing and litigation of trademarks; providing a website featuring information about intellectual property services relating to search, registration, prosecution, maintenance and monitoring of trademarks" (U.S. Registration No. 6228449). The second application was filed under class 41 for "Educational services in the field of intellectual property legal topics and distribution of educational materials in connection therewith" (U.S. Serial No. 97732908).

For each class of goods for which trademark registration is sought, the USPTO requires a separate filing fee be paid at the time the application is filed. The application must also specify the filing basis for each class. If the class identification is inaccurate, you will never be able to submit a specimen to support the use of the mark with those goods or services. This results in additional expenses and wastes time, as it will be necessary to file a new trademark application to correct and properly identify the classification. Also, the USPTO will reject the application if you do not include a specific enough description of the goods or services associated with the mark.

SPECIMEN OF USE IN COMMERCE

If the trademark application is filed based on use in commerce, a specimen of the use also needs to be submitted at the time of filing. The specimen is evidence of how the mark is actually being used in commerce. A specimen is required for each class of goods or services that is identified in the application. The following are examples of the types of specimens that can be used for a trademark associated with the sale of goods: labels, hangtags, packaging, photos of the trademark used on the goods, and websites through which the goods may be purchased. The following are examples of the types of specimens used for services: websites and advertising brochures. Unacceptable specimens are drawings and digitally created or altered specimens.

TRADEMARK APPLICATION TIMELINE AND SERIAL NUMBER

As of the writing of this book, the trademark application process, from the time of filing the application to receiving a registered mark from the USPTO, averages between 12 and 18 months. The length of time varies based on numerous factors. Of course, the fewer issues there are with the trademark application, the faster the application will be processed.

When you file a trademark application, the USPTO assigns it a unique serial number to identify it. The serial number is assigned regardless of whether a trademark application is approved or not. After the application is filed, the next step is for the application to be assigned to a U.S. trademark examiner to review the application. Approximately six to nine months after the application is filed, depending on how busy the USPTO is, the USPTO will either issue an office action (discussed in chapter nine) or approve and publish the trademark.

NOTICE OF PUBLICATION

Receiving a notice of publication from the USPTO is great news because it indicates preliminary approval of your trademark and means you are now one step closer to registration. However, receiving a notice of publication is still not a guarantee that your trademark will ultimately be registered. Rather, once published, the public will be on notice, and it is possible for others to oppose the application. Pending trademarks are published for opposition in the USPTO's *Trademark Official Gazette* (*TMOG* or *Official Gazette*). The *Official Gazette* is a weekly online publication that gives notice to the public that the USPTO intends to register certain trademarks. A trademark is published in the *Official Gazette* approximately one month after approval.

Once published, anyone who believes their business will be harmed by the registration of the trademark may, within 30 days from the date of publication, file an objection to the registration

(called an "opposition"). An opposition is an administrative proceeding held before the Trademark Trial and Appeal Board (TTAB)
that can extend the timeline of your trademark application. If an
experienced IP attorney is representing you, they have docketing
systems in place and get alerts in the event an opposition is filed.
In addition, as counsel of record, your attorney will be notified
if an opposition proceeding commences. When this happens, the
USPTO takes no further action to register your trademark until
the 30-day opposition period has ended and any oppositions are
resolved.

Approximately three months after your trademark is published in the *Official Gazette*, if no opposition is filed, the USPTO
registers your trademark. If an opposition was filed but was unsuc-
cessful, the USPTO will register your trademark after the TTAB
dismisses the opposition.

STATEMENT OF USE

The difference between a use-based and intent-to-use application
in relation to the process described above is what happens after
the notice of allowance is issued. As previously mentioned, within
six months of the date of issuance of the notice of allowance, you
will need to either file a Statement of Use, wherein you provide the
date of first use anywhere and the date of first use in commerce
along with at least one specimen of the use, or file a request for extension of time (remember the discussions above regarding being
able to file up to a total of five six-month extensions of time and
the date of first use anywhere and date of first use in commerce).

After the USPTO reviews the Statement of Use, the USPTO
will either issue an office action identifying deficiencies that need
to be resolved before issuing the registration or approve the SOU

and register the trademark. If the SOU is approved, registration typically occurs within two months.

Notably, a study done in 2013 revealed that 80 percent of published marks never obtained registration status because the applicants did not file the required Statement of Use showing that they began using the mark with the goods or services specified in the application.[85]

YOU ARE MORE LIKELY TO OBTAIN A REGISTERED TRADEMARK WHEN AN EXPERIENCED TRADEMARK ATTORNEY REPRESENTS YOU

You may be wondering whether you are more likely to have your trademark application approved if you use a trademark attorney. The answer is a resounding YES! Statistics reveal that an applicant has a greater chance of their mark being published and ultimately registered if an experienced trademark attorney is engaged to represent them in the application process.[86] In fact, applicants have an almost 20 percent greater chance of getting to the publication stage (that means overcoming any office action objections) when represented by counsel.[87] Based on a study done in 2013, an inexperienced *pro se* (meaning, not represented by an attorney) applicant had only a 40 percent chance of registration after receiving an office action, whereas applicants who had an experienced attorney representing them through an office action had a 60 percent likelihood of registration.[88]

If you are serious about getting a federal trademark registration, it would not be in your best interest to proceed with filing a trademark application without experienced counsel to assist you. As you can see, there are numerous areas in the process where it is easy to make mistakes (that you may not even realize you are making). Many mistakes can be overcome and handled, allowing the application to move toward publication and registration of the mark, if addressed sooner versus later. So, do not be discouraged if you have filed an application yourself and received an office action. The message here is to act now and retain experienced counsel to assist you.

There are numerous reasons why the USPTO rejects trademark applications. In the next chapter, I will discuss those most common.

CHAPTER 9

Common Reasons for Trademark Application Refusal

I will discuss the rejection of trademark applications in greater depth in this chapter. As mentioned previously, the basis of refusal is addressed in the form of an office action issued by a USPTO trademark examiner. In addition, a third party may file a trademark opposition, objecting to the issuance of a trademark registration.

OFFICE ACTIONS

In an office action, a trademark examiner will identify problems with the application and explain the grounds for refusing to register your trademark. The examiner will then give you an opportunity to respond to and present arguments and additional information to address or correct the issues that are preventing registration. For office actions issued on or after December 3, 2022, an applicant must respond within three months from the date the office action was issued. One three-month extension of time may be requested for a fee. While an applicant may respond to an office action without being represented by an attorney, it is prudent to engage an attorney to respond on your behalf. Your chances of overcoming the office action increase when you are represented by an experienced trademark attorney.[89] Recall the discussion at the end of chapter eight addressing the benefits of engaging an attorney to assist you in the trademark registration process.

If you fail to respond to the office action in a timely manner, the USPTO will deem your application abandoned, which means the USPTO will label the application as dead in its database. The USPTO will also issue a Notice of Abandonment and the application will no longer be able to be processed; thus, your trademark will not be registered.

PETITIONS TO REVIVE AFTER ABANDONMENT

You can revive an application within two months of the issuance of a Notice of Abandonment by filing a petition to revive and submitting the petition fee. If the petition is filed later than two months after the abandonment date, it will be denied as untimely. If you did not receive the Notice of Abandonment, a petition to revive may be filed within two months of learning of the abandonment and no later than six months after the date of the abandonment. If the petition to revive deadlines are missed and you still wish to pursue federal registration of your mark, the only option at that point is to file a new trademark application. If you file a new trademark application, the whole process starts over again.

If you file a response to an office action and it does not overcome all the issues identified, the examining attorney will issue a "final" office action that makes final the remaining refusals or requirements. At that point, you generally have two options: (1) appeal the trademark examiner's decision by filing an appeal with the Trademark Trial and Appeal Board or (2) submit a timely response to the final office action wherein you overcome the remaining objections. If you fail to take either of these steps, the USPTO will deem the trademark application abandoned, and your trademark will not be registered. If you are faced with either of these two scenarios, while a trademark applicant may proceed *pro se*, it is not recommended. By proceeding without an attorney, you would be at greater risk of not being able to overcome the office action.

SUCCESS STORY

I once received a call from a woman who was in a panic. She had filed trademark applications without using an attorney, received an office action, and had attempted to respond without the assistance of an attorney. It was down to the wire for her to respond to a final office action by the deadline. She was afraid her trademark applications would be abandoned if she did not respond in a timely manner and do so correctly. Fortunately, I was able to jump in and review her applications, correct some unintentional mistakes she had made, and then quickly respond to the office action. Shortly after doing so, we received the good news that we had successfully overcome the office action and that her applications were on a solid foundation to proceed to the next step of the registration process. The client was able to breathe a sigh of relief, and she was grateful that I was able to preserve her trademark rights and prevent her marks from being abandoned. Notably, even if the client overcame the office action on her own, resulting in the mark proceeding to registration, if the mark was challenged down the road, she would have lost her trademark rights due to her unknowingly providing incorrect information to the USPTO as part of her trademark application.

COMMON REASONS FOR TRADEMARK REFUSAL

Common reasons for a trademark application to be refused include likelihood of confusion; being merely descriptive of goods or services; being geographically descriptive or misdescriptive of the origin of the goods or services; the specimen not supporting use for the described goods or services; using merely a surname, title of a single creative work, or character name; or the trademark being used in an ornamental manner. This chapter will also address trademark opposition proceedings in more detail.

Likelihood of Confusion

Likelihood of confusion is the most common basis for the USPTO to refuse to register a mark during its review of a trademark application.[90] Also known as a Section 2(d) refusal, this type of refusal is based on finding a likelihood of confusion between the mark in the application and a mark that is pending registration or was registered before with the USPTO. As with all refusals, an applicant who receives a likelihood of confusion refusal may submit arguments and evidence in response to the office action to attempt to overcome the refusal without the need to pay an additional fee. However, if the response is not filed in a timely manner, it does not matter how persuasive the applicant's arguments are or how compelling the evidence submitted is because the mark will be refused and deemed to have been abandoned.

Merely Descriptive

Another common basis for refusal by the USPTO is that the trademark examiner finds the proposed mark merely descriptive of the goods or services in the application. This is referred to as a Section 2(e)(1) refusal. An applicant may attempt to overcome the refusal and obtain registration of the mark by filing a timely response to the office action.

Remember, in chapter six, I explained that a descriptive trademark cannot be registered on the Principal Register. To obtain federal trademark protection, a term must be distinctive and not merely descriptive. This means the term must be capable of identifying a single source of goods or services, even if that source is unknown. Distinctiveness may be either inherent or acquired. Inherently distinctive means the mark immediately identifies the source of a specific product or service. A merely descriptive mark is not inherently distinctive because consumers do not view the mark as identifying the source of the goods or services with which it is associated. An example of a descriptive mark is the term *handy repairs* used for repair services. Go back to chapter six for more examples of descriptive trademarks.

Here is the good news: a merely descriptive common law trademark may acquire distinctiveness over time. This occurs when consumers associate the mark with a single source of goods or services, generally through use of the mark over time (at least five years). If a term has acquired distinctiveness (also referred to as secondary meaning), it may be protected as an enforceable trademark and registered on the Principal Register. If an applicant cannot demonstrate that a merely descriptive term has secondary meaning at the time the trademark application is filed, the mark may nevertheless be able to be registered on the Supplemental Register.

To determine whether the proposed mark is merely descriptive versus inherently distinctive, the trademark examiner considers whether the mark conveys knowledge of an ingredient, quality, characteristic, feature, function, purpose, or use of the goods or service. This is not analyzed in the abstract. Rather, the trademark examiner must consider the proposed mark in relationship to the particular goods or services for which the applicant seeks registration and the context in which the mark is being used.

Notably, a mark does not need to immediately convey an idea of each and every specific feature of the goods or services to be found merely descriptive. The trademark examiner could refuse the proposed mark as merely descriptive even if the mark describes only one significant attribute, function, or property of the goods.[91] So, it is generally best to limit descriptive terms in your mark or combine the terms with a unique logo to increase your chances of obtaining a registered trademark.

Foreign Words

If your trademark contains foreign terms, the trademark examiner will translate words from the foreign language into English before analyzing the words for descriptiveness. A word that is descriptive in a foreign language is usually deemed descriptive in English. Notably, a combination of foreign and English words may result in a distinctive mark if the commercial impression created sufficiently differs from the literal translation.

For example, the literal translation of the mark La Yogurt is The Yogurt. Although the USPTO initially refused registration because the term was merely a generic word, the applicant appealed the examiner's decision to the TTAB. The TTAB reversed the refusal, finding instead that the mark was inherently distinctive because the French article *La* combined with the generic English word *yogurt* altered the commercial impression of the overall mark.[92]

Surnames

If your mark is merely a surname, an examining attorney could issue an office action refusing registration. Whether a mark is "merely" a surname depends on the primary significance of the mark to the relevant purchasing public. The trademark examiner decides each case on its own merits and resolves any doubt in favor of the applicant.[93]

Factors that may be considered include: (1) the degree of the surname's rarity, (2) whether anyone connected with the applicant has the same surname, (3) whether the surname has a meaning unrelated to the surname, (4) whether the surname has the structure and pronunciation of a surname, and (5) the effect of any stylization of the words or stylistic elements.[94] When the proposed mark has a meaning that is recognized apart from its surname significance, this reduces the likelihood consumers will perceive the mark as primarily a surname. Thus, one way the applicant can attempt to overcome a surname refusal is to submit arguments in favor of other meanings for the disputed term. To do so, the applicant will need to provide evidence the mark has an alternative, non-surname meaning. For example, the TTAB has upheld a trademark examiner's refusal when the term was the business founder's surname and the applicant failed to submit evidence to support the term being an acronym.[95]

Geographically Descriptive or Deceptively Misdescriptive

If the proposed mark is primarily geographically descriptive or primarily geographically deceptively misdescriptive of the goods or services, a trademark examiner may issue an office action refusing registration. Again, the applicant may attempt to overcome the refusal by submitting arguments and evidence to the USPTO.

For example, the USPTO refused registration of the mark Minnesota Cigar Company for cigars made in Minnesota.[96] The trademark examiner determined the mark was primarily geographically descriptive and refused registration because (1) the primary significance of the mark was a generally known geographic location, (2) the goods or services identified in the trademark application came from the place identified by the mark, and (3) purchasers of the goods or services were likely to believe the goods originated in the place identified by the mark (that is, Minnesota).

Like other merely descriptive marks, if the examiner allows the mark to be registered, a geographically descriptive mark can eventually be registered on the Principal Register if it acquires distinctiveness while on the Supplemental Register. A refusal based on the mark being geographically deceptively misdescriptive requires that the trademark examiner show public deception. For example, the TTAB refused registration of the mark Old Havana for rum based on it being geographically deceptively misdescriptive because the rum was not made in Cuba, and consumers would recognize Old Havana as a city in Cuba.[97]

Specimen Not Supporting Use

Another common refusal for a trademark application is when the examiner finds that the specimen does not support use in commerce for the goods or services identified in the application. If you do not have a specimen supporting the trademark use, the mark will not be approved for registration.

Book Titles/Single Works

People often confuse trademarks, copyrights, and patents. In other words, people often use these words interchangeably as though they are one and the same. I am routinely asked whether the title of a book can be protected with a trademark registration. The simple answer is no, a book title cannot be trademarked. You will not be able to register the words with the USPTO if they are used as the title of a single creative work. There is, however, an exception. If the book is part of a series of creative works, it may be able to be registered with the USPTO because it serves as a brand identifier. For example, the book title *The Tipping Point* identifies a single book, whereas National Public Radio's *All Things Considered* radio program is a series because there is more than one creative work under that name. Other common examples of series of books are the *For Dummies* and *Chicken Soup for the Soul* books.

Fictional Characters

The name of a fictional character cannot be trademarked to protect the name in and of itself; however, the name and likeness of a fictional character may be trademarked if it is used to brand your goods or services. The use can be established by selling products with the character's image or using the character in advertising associated with your goods or services. Well-known examples of character trademarks are Disney's Mickey Mouse and the Pillsbury Doughboy.

Ornamental and Decorative Marks

If a trademark is used in an ornamental or decorative manner, you will not be able to obtain trademark registration. So, what is ornamental use, you may be wondering? When use does not clearly identify the source of the good and distinguish your goods from other goods. For example, a logo on the front of a baseball cap. The logo is associated with an organization—perhaps a sports team—that did not manufacture the hat. Another example is a quote or a symbol displayed across the front of a T-shirt, as most purchasers would perceive this as a decoration and would not think it identified the company that manufactured the T-shirt. The source of the T-shirt, as reflected on the tag, could be Hanes®, for example.

TRADEMARK OPPOSITION PROCEEDINGS

A trademark opposition proceeding is a type of proceeding before the TTAB filed by a third party (often a competitor or another business) who is objecting to the applicant obtaining a federal registration for their trademark. Generally, the third party believes that if the USPTO grants federal trademark rights to the pending mark, their own mark or business interests may be harmed or damaged in some way.

There are various reasons a third party may commence an opposition proceeding to prevent you from obtaining a registered trademark. Unfortunately, in my experience, there is not always a good basis for a third party to initiate an opposition proceeding. The third party may do so for competitive advantage; for instance, companies with deep pockets may file trademark opposition proceedings in an attempt to protect their own trademark portfolios. Some third parties believe that filing the opposition creates leverage to get the applicant to withdraw their application and come to an amicable resolution.

RIGHT TO APPEAL

If you are not able to overcome a refusal by the USPTO, you have the right to appeal the decision before the TTAB. There are hard deadlines that must be met when you appeal an adverse office action or disallowance decision. If you believe the TTAB erred in its appellate decision, you may attempt to seek further recourse before the Federal Circuit Court of Appeals by filing a lawsuit. In doing so, the Federal Circuit Court will review the case and issue a judicial decision on the matter. An experienced attorney can review your matter and determine whether you have a basis for appealing the adverse trademark decision.

If you are successful in getting past the office actions and any opposition proceedings, and your trademark becomes registered, congratulations! However, you must still be proactive in maintaining your trademark by complying with all of the USPTO's trademark maintenance requirements. In the following chapter, I will discuss these compliance requirements and explain the steps a trademark owner needs to follow to keep their registration live at the USPTO.

CHAPTER 10

Trademark Maintenance Responsibilities

IN MY EXPERIENCE, BUSINESS OWNERS OFTEN MISTAKENLY BELIEVE that once they obtain a trademark registration from the USPTO, there are no requirements to maintain those rights. This is simply not the case. There are ongoing requirements to maintain your trademark rights. In fact, if a trademark owner fails to do what is necessary, their trademark rights can be lost. Trademark rights are not indefinite and must be maintained to be kept. In this chapter, I discuss a registered trademark owner's responsibility to ensure ongoing trademark protection.

CONTINUOUS AND CONSISTENT TRADEMARK USE IS REQUIRED

First, to maintain trademark registration, the trademark owner must continuously and consistently use the trademark in commerce in connection with the goods or services identified in the registration. Consistent use means using the mark exactly as indicated in the trademark registration. If the trademark owner moves away from using the mark in association with the goods or services identified in the registration and instead begins to use the mark in association with other goods or services, this "new" type of use will not be viewed as continuous use. Here is a practice pointer: schedule regular reviews of your trademarks to ensure that the way you use them does not change over time. It is very important to regularly monitor how your marks are being used in commerce to ensure that the trademark use is consistent with the registration.

To help you stay organized in reviewing how you are using your trademarks, I have created a trademark review form that you may use in your business. See the resources in the Additional Information section at the back of this book for a link to the copy of this tool.

If a mark is not used for three or more years and the trademark owner has no intention of using the trademark again in the future, the lack of use of the mark can result in the cancellation of trademark rights or the mark being deemed abandoned (to be discussed in chapter 11).

By contrast, if the trademark continues to be used in commerce but use of the mark has changed or expanded beyond the use of goods or services stated in the registration, then it is generally advisable for the trademark owner to file a new trademark application to identify and disclose the new classes of goods or services in order to protect the mark's expanded scope of use. If a new application related to a trademark you already secured for other classes of goods or services is filed for new classes, it will start the trademark application process over again. Expanding a trademark to new classes cannot be done by merely adding a new class as part of a renewal application. A new application for the expanded use is required. It is possible that a trademark owner could be successful in obtaining a trademark in one class but not in another class. Thus, before you decide to expand the use of a trademark in your portfolio, I recommend that you conduct a new trademark search (as discussed in chapter seven) to investigate whether your mark is available for its new expanded use, minimizing the risk of infringing on another company's rights.

When litigation is brought for trademark infringement, a common defense asserted by purported trademark infringers is that the mark was abandoned and, as a result, the claimant does not have any trademark rights. Overcoming this type of defense can become a very expensive and stressful battle, especially when a trademark owner has stopped using the mark for at least three years. In fact, if a company stops using its trademark for an extended period of time with no intent to use the mark in the future, the business that was initially accused of trademark infringement can end up being awarded senior trademark rights.

The analysis will come down to the specific facts and circumstances of each case; however, the entire situation can be avoided if trademark use is regularly monitored. If there are any changes regarding the use of your mark, it is better to be safe than sorry and confer with a trademark attorney to determine whether or not a new trademark application should be filed to capture and protect any new or expanded use of your trademarks.

MAINTENANCE AND RENEWAL FILINGS

In addition to continuously using the mark in commerce, the USPTO has maintenance filing requirements that must be complied with. If those requirements are not met, a trademark owner will lose their rights and the mark will be deemed abandoned and reflected as dead in the USPTO database, even if the trademark owner is still using the mark.

USPTO Section 8 Declaration

The first USPTO maintenance filing requirement occurs between the fifth and sixth years after the mark was initially registered. The trademark owner is required to file what's referred to as a Section 8 declaration, wherein they are required to attest to how the trademark is being used or, alternatively, provide information to support "excusable nonuse" of a mark. Excusable nonuse of a mark occurs when the mark's nonuse is due to circumstances beyond the trademark owner's control: for example, a trade embargo. Regardless of the reason for the nonuse, at a minimum, the trademark owner must be able to show that they had no intention to abandon the mark.

Examples of where the USPTO may not consider the reason for nonuse to be a valid excuse include nonuse resulting from a business decision and nonuse resulting from a decrease in consumer demand for the goods or services associated with the mark for an indefinite period of time.

According to the legal requirements for a complete declaration, "If the registered mark is not in use in commerce on or in connection with all the goods, services, or classes specified in the registration," [98] the declaration must state the date when the use in commerce stopped and include the approximate date when use is expected to resume. Further, the declaration must include "facts to show that the nonuse . . . is due to special circumstances that excuse the nonuse and is not due to an intention to abandon the mark."[99]

In addition to filing the Section 8 declaration and paying the required fee, the trademark owner will also need to submit an updated specimen reflecting the current use of the mark in commerce in association with the goods or services identified in the registration to the USPTO. There is a six-month grace period after the six-year anniversary of registering to file the Section 8 declaration (for an additional fee). If the trademark owner fails to timely file the Section 8 declaration, the USPTO will cancel the registration.

The takeaway is this: first, if you own a trademark, you should continue to use the mark in commerce as long it makes sense to do so; second, if you are unable to continue to use the mark in commerce, be prepared to explain the reasons for the mark's non-use to the USPTO. Often, your nonuse will be deemed "excusable," allowing you to maintain your right to the mark. In either case, however, it is very important to continue to timely file the required maintenance documents to keep the trademark active with the USPTO. If you are unsure of how to file a Section 8 declaration or need assistance doing so, engage a trademark attorney for help.

USPTO Section 15 Declaration of Incontestability

If your trademark is registered on the Principal Register and you have continuously used the mark in commerce for at least five consecutive years following the date of registration for all of the goods or services identified in the registration, you are eligible to file a Section 15 declaration of incontestability at the time of filing the Section 8 declaration. By filing a Section 15 declaration, the owner of the mark claims incontestable rights to the trademark. When a trademark is deemed incontestable by the USPTO, it will have heightened defenses in the event a trademark dispute arises, and your ownership and exclusive rights to use the mark will be deemed incontestable. The principal benefit of having an "incontestable" mark is that you will not be burdened with having to prove to others that you are entitled to exclusive rights.

Although there is an additional fee, I highly recommend that my clients file Section 8 and 15 declarations together (assuming they satisfy the filing requirements), as there are benefits to doing so. Unlike the Section 8 declaration, however, there is no dead-line to file a Section 15 declaration, so it can be filed at any time following eligibility. It is important to note, though, that a mark registered on the Supplemental Register is not eligible for incontestability status. For example, a merely descriptive trademark does not initially qualify for incontestability status because the mark can only be registered on the Supplemental Register until it acquires distinctiveness or secondary meaning and becomes registered on the Principal Register (see discussions about the Principal and Supplemental Registers in chapter five and distinctive trademarks in chapter six).

After the Section 15 declaration is filed and accepted, the USPTO deems the trademark incontestable. This means there are certain aspects of the registration that cannot be challenged by third parties. This is a heightened protection. The word *incontestable* does not mean the mark cannot be challenged in the future. However, incontestable status can give a trademark owner leverage when dealing with an infringer because this status provides conclusive evidence of the strength of the mark; so, this alone can be a deterrent against potential infringers who want to challenge the strength and validity of your trademark.

Once a trademark receives incontestable status, the registration of the trademark is deemed conclusive evidence of the validity of the trademark, the owner's ownership of the trademark, and the owner's exclusive right to use the mark with the goods or services identified in the registration.

Renewal Documents Must Be Filed Every Ten Years

The next filing requirement with the USPTO occurs between the ninth and tenth year after the initial trademark registration date and then reoccurs every ten years thereafter. With each renewal document filed with the USPTO, the trademark owner is required to also file a specimen showing the current use of the mark in commerce.

If a company is sold to a new entity and the trademark rights are included in the sale, or if a trademark was inherited, it may be necessary to file an assignment document with the USPTO so that the records correctly reflect the proper owner of the mark. If the owner of the mark has changed, the new mark owner steps into the shoes of the prior mark owner and, as a result, assumes responsibility for ensuring the mark is being properly maintained, including being the party who is required to file maintenance documents on the same timeline that applied to the prior mark owner.

Although a trademark owner is not required to submit a specimen showing the use of each and every good or service identified in the registration, but rather only a specimen for each class of goods or services, it is necessary that the trademark owner be able to submit a specimen related to any good or service referenced if requested by the USPTO. For example, if the class of goods is clothing and the types of articles are shirts, pants, and ties, it is not necessary to file a specimen reflecting the use of each type, but be prepared to provide such a specimen if requested by the USPTO.

In this regard, the USPTO started the Post Registration Audit Program in 2017 to randomly audit registrations and maintenance filings. The intention of the program is to promote the accuracy and integrity of trademark registrations.[100] If the USPTO audits your maintenance filing, you will need to prove use of the trademark for additional goods or services identified in the registration. If you are subjected to this type of audit, it is in your best interest to engage a trademark attorney to guide you through the process so you do not unintentionally jeopardize your trademark rights.

TRADEMARK MONITORING

A misconception I find that trademark owners often have is believing that once they have secured a registered trademark from the USPTO, they are automatically protected from potential infringers. This is not true. Brand protection involves monitoring the market to make sure competitors are not using the same or similar brand identifiers to sell similar goods or services and being prepared to take action to enforce your company's rights if an issue is identified. It is incumbent upon the trademark owner to police and monitor their marks to ensure that no other entity is using their brand names without permission to sell unauthorized goods or services.

Infringement comes in many different forms. If a third party is using your mark or a mark that is confusingly similar to your mark to sell their goods or services or, worse yet, market and sell counterfeit or knockoff goods, it is your responsibility as the owner to take action to stop the third party from continuing to use your trademark. The following example underscores this important point.

Counterfeiting Scenario

If an entity or individual sells knockoff Louis Vuitton handbags, that entity or individual exposes themselves to liability for trademark infringement, which carries with it, if proven, huge financial penalties along with potential criminal penalties. Under the

Trademark Counterfeiting Act, a trademark infringer potentially exposes themself to penalties of up to ten years in prison and $2 million in fines if they intentionally "[traffic] in goods or services and knowingly [use] a counterfeit mark on or in connection with such goods or services," or "[traffic] in labels, . . . documentation, or packaging . . . knowing that a counterfeit mark has been applied thereto."[101] This is serious stuff, and, clearly, the penalties can be life-changing.

Unfortunately, most companies, in my experience, do not appreciate these risks until it is too late. Instead of implementing monitoring systems and processes to protect their intellectual property assets, many companies leave it to chance to learn about potential infringers.

Consumer Confusion Scenario

Imagine you own a company that has built a strong brand, and your customer base is growing faster than you expected. Word is out that your brand can be trusted for its high-quality products and good customer service. However, what you have failed to do is implement safeguards to alert you of potential brand infringers. Perhaps you figure "it won't happen to me." Then one day, just by chance, you come across a competitor's website that is using your company's logo. Ugh! Or perhaps you discovered the infringer because you receive a call from a potential customer who confused your company with the competitor's company. Or, perhaps worse yet, you receive a call from an irate customer who hired a competitor, mistakenly thinking it was your company, and its services were terrible! Now the customer is blaming you and demanding their money back when your company did not even provide the service.

These scenarios are compelling evidence that the risk of likelihood of confusion is real, and they underscore why you should
proactively monitor your brand. It is imprudent to leave your
trademark watch to chance. You can lose your trademark rights by
not policing the use of your mark. If a mark is not surveilled, it is
in danger of attack and can end up being worthless.

Therefore, the best practice is to engage a brand protection
attorney to help you police your mark by implementing a comprehensive trademark watch designed to search a broad spectrum of
sources, review and analyze the information obtained, and alert
you of any issues that require action. When my clients request this
service, I conduct a comprehensive trademark watch that includes
searches of state and federal databases to capture newly filed
trademark applications as well as applications that are published
in the USPTO's *Official Gazette*. Monitoring trademark filing
activity at the USPTO can be extremely beneficial. For instance,
being able to identify an objectionable trademark application
when it is filed with the USPTO could give a trademark owner the
opportunity to object before the applicant has invested a large sum
of resources in the mark, especially in the case of an intent-to-use
application where the applicant has not yet used the mark in commerce. An early objection can increase the chances of a favorable
outcome and potentially avoid a costly and protracted opposition
proceeding.

It is also important to structure a trademark watch to search
domain names, social media platforms, and other market and
industry sources for infringing marks. A trademark attorney will
be able to guide you on how frequently such a report should be
generated based on your mark and the nature of your business.
Generally, trademark watch reports are generated monthly or

quarterly. If you decide not to hire a trademark attorney to help you monitor your mark, I urge you to conduct frequent searches and routinely monitor the market for potential infringers on your own so you can quickly respond to issues.

There also are nonattorney services that provide watch services; however, it is advisable that the search be overseen by a trademark attorney who will be able to help construct the search parameters and interpret the information.

Regardless of how you choose to proceed in monitoring your mark, I recommend that, at a minimum, you include the cost of a trademark watch or monitoring service as part of your trademark maintenance budget. It is a small expense that can provide tremendous peace of mind. Maintaining your trademark rights is key, and this requires ongoing action on your part.

Even if you properly maintain your trademarks as discussed in this chapter, there are still circumstances where your trademark rights may be challenged and ultimately canceled. I will discuss trademark cancellation proceedings in the next chapter.

CHAPTER 11

Trademark Cancellation Proceedings

I PREVIOUSLY DISCUSSED TRADEMARK OPPOSITION PROCEEDINGS, and in this chapter, I will address trademark cancellation proceedings. While an opposition proceeding is filed by a third party who is trying to block the registration of a particular trademark during the application process, cancellation proceedings occur after a trademark is registered. Like opposition proceedings, cancellation proceedings also take place before the Trademark Trial and Appeal Board of the United States Patent and Trademark Office.

A cancellation proceeding is common when a trademark registration blocks or poses a threat of blocking a third party's application for the same or similar mark. There are various grounds for seeking the cancellation of a trademark. These include abandonment, fraud, nonuse, genericness, likelihood of confusion, and dilution.

You may be wondering how these cancellation proceedings can occur if the USPTO approves a trademark for registration. Here's the answer: the TTAB's jurisdiction is limited to determining the rights to register trademarks. For example, the likelihood of confusion argument may be raised by a third party who was not aware of the trademark application or the existence of a confusingly similar mark until after it was registered. Remember, if the third party was doing the necessary trademark monitoring, as discussed in chapter ten, they could file an opposition proceeding and block the registration. When there are direct hits during a trademark search, meaning the search found an identical trademark for similar goods or services that was previously applied for or is registered, the trademark examiner will usually flag this in an office action. However, sometimes there is a trademark that is not identical to the applied-for mark, and it is not picked up by the examiner.

I represented a client who experienced this situation. The examiner was unaware of my client's mark because it was not picked up in the examiner's search. Although the mark was similar, it was not identical. In that situation, we were able to submit what is called a letter of protest, requesting that the alleged confusingly similar mark be brought to the attention of the examiner. Letters of protest are sent to and reviewed by the deputy commissioner's office of the USPTO to determine whether to forward the information to the examining attorney for review. If the letter of protest does not pass the approval of the deputy commissioner, it is not recorded in the trademark proceeding or forwarded to the examining attorney. In the case I handled, the letter of protest was forwarded to the examining attorney, who had already issued an unrelated office action. The trademark applicant did not respond to the outstanding office action, and the trademark application was abandoned.

Unlike a federal court litigation proceeding, where these same arguments may be raised, a TTAB proceeding will not result in a determination of the rights to use a trademark, nor will it result in a determination as to issues of infringement or unfair competition;

issuance of an order for injunctive relief; or an award of damages, attorneys' fees, or costs.

In light of the complexity of trademark law and practice before the TTAB, it is highly recommended that parties hire an attorney to represent them in these proceedings. Unlike in federal court, where corporate entities are required to be represented by counsel, U.S. parties in an opposition proceeding may appear *pro se* (without counsel).[102] However, it is advisable not to do so because it may negatively impact the likelihood of your success. On the other hand, a foreign-domiciled party must be represented by a United States licensed attorney in a TTAB proceeding. A party is deemed foreign-domiciled if it is an individual with a permanent legal residence outside the United States or its territories, or an entity with its principal place of business (in other words, its headquarters) outside the United States or its territories.[103] If a foreign-domiciled entity sells its branded goods or services in the United States, it would have an interest in securing exclusive rights to use its brand assets in the United States in the same way that a U.S. entity would want to secure its rights in the U.S.

ABANDONMENT

An action of abandonment can be commenced when a third party seeks registration of a trademark believing the trademark owner has discontinued use of the mark in connection with the goods or services identified in the registration. In doing so, the third party may claim the applicant has engaged in nonuse of the mark or submitted a fraudulent declaration of use to the USPTO as part of the renewal filings. Remember, if a mark is not used in commerce in connection with the goods or services identified in the registration for a period exceeding three years or if there is evidence that the mark owner does not intend to resume use of the mark in connection with the goods or services, the USPTO can deem the mark abandoned. A factual scenario where this may be applicable is where a company is no longer operating and, therefore, is no longer using the trademark.

FRAUD AND NONUSE

A cancellation proceeding for fraud or nonuse of a mark may be commenced by a third party who is using or intends to use the same or a similar mark. Sometimes, the third party will have already filed a trademark application for the mark in question, and the trademark examiner has issued an office action citing likelihood of confusion with the registered mark as a basis for refusal of the registration. In fact, this may be what prompted the third party to file the cancellation proceeding. Or the proceeding could have been prompted by the trademark owner sending a cease and desist letter to the third party.

In a cancellation proceeding for fraud or nonuse, the third party essentially claims that the trademark owner's representations to the USPTO were false at the time they were made and is therefore requesting the USPTO cancel the trademark registration. For example, if a trademark owner was in fact not using the mark associated with all the goods or services identified in the registration at the time they stated they started using the trademark, or they made representations that were false in the trademark renewal applications, this could serve as a basis for a third party cancellation proceeding. If a trademark is canceled, the mark owner will lose their federal trademark rights; however, they may still have common law rights in particular geographic territories.

GENERICIDE

In trademark law, there is a concept called "genericide." Genericide occurs when a trademarked term is so frequently and commonly used in the public domain that, as a result, the term becomes generic. If this occurs, a trademark will not be enforceable, and the trademark owner will lose their rights. Once you review the following examples, the concept will make more sense to you.

There are several well-known brands that lost their trademark rights because their marks became so commonly used that they lost their distinctiveness and became generic terms for particular products or services. In other words, the marks no longer served as source identifiers of the products or services but rather became common household words. "A mark is generic if its primary significance to the relevant public is the class or category of goods or services on or in connection with which it is used" as opposed to being an indicator of a source.[104] This concept is referred to as genericide or genericization.

Here are some examples that illustrate genericide. The term *escalator*, for example, was trademarked by Otis Elevator Company for their moving staircases. However, due to widespread usage of the term (which was not policed or sufficiently policed), the word became generic and is now commonly used to describe any moving staircase manufactured by any company. Otis Elevator Company lost its trademark rights to the term escalator in 1950.[105]

The term *aspirin* was once a trademark owned by the pharmaceutical company Bayer. However, over time, the term aspirin became so commonly used to refer to any pain reliever (regardless of specific brand) that Bayer lost its trademark rights.[106]

Another example is the term *thermos*. The term was registered as a trademark in 1907 by the American Thermos Bottle Company.

However, because the American Thermos Bottle Company did not effectively police the use of the word thermos as a brand identifier, the word became commonly used as a generic term for any vacuum bottle.[107] As a result, the American Thermos Bottle Company lost its trademark rights.

These examples demonstrate how important it is for trademark owners to be proactive in protecting their trademarks to prevent them from becoming generic. Genericide happens over time, and there are actions a trademark owner can take to help avoid the issue. As previously discussed, policing one's mark is key. In addition to engaging in efforts to uncover unauthorized use of the same or a similar mark, you can prevent brand genericide by stopping the use of the trademarked terms as nouns or verbs.

For instance, in 2017, Google won a genericide trademark case. In that case, the plaintiff claimed the term *Google* had become a generic verb to describe the process of searching for something on the internet using any type of search engine. The court held that although *Google* is frequently used as a verb, it is still a brand source identifier because the company remains distinct and is viewed by consumers as the designated source of services.[108]

LIKELIHOOD OF CONFUSION

Likelihood of confusion and dilution are two additional common reasons the USPTO cancels trademarks, and these claims are often asserted together. Under the Lanham Act, a trademark is not entitled to registration if it is similar enough to a previously used or registered mark that it is likely to cause consumer confusion, mistake, or deception about the source of origin of the goods or services.[109] Accordingly, a third party may attempt to cancel a registration based on the fact the registered mark is likely to be confused with an earlier registered mark. The TTAB evaluates likelihood of confusion claims using the multifactor test set forth in the *In re E.I. DuPont de Nemours & Co.* case (often referred to as the DuPont factors).[110] The DuPont factors are as follows:

(1) The similarity or dissimilarity of the marks in their entireties as to appearance, sound, connotation, and commercial impression.

(2) The similarity or dissimilarity and nature of the goods or services as described in an application or registration or in connection with which a prior mark is in use.

(3) The similarity or dissimilarity of established, likely-to-continue trade channels.

(4) The conditions under which and buyers to whom sales are made, i.e., "impulse" vs. careful, sophisticated purchasing.

(5) The fame of the prior mark (sales, advertising, length of use).

(6) The number and nature of similar marks in use on similar goods.

(7) The nature and extent of any actual confusion.

(8) The length of time during and conditions under which there has been concurrent use without evidence of actual confusion.

(9) The variety of goods on which a mark is or is not used (house mark, "family" mark, product mark).

(10) The market interface between applicant and the owner of a prior mark:
   (a) a mere "consent" to register or use.
   (b) agreement provisions designed to preclude confusion, i.e., limitations on continued use of the marks by each party.
   (c) assignment of mark, application, registration and good will of the related businesses.
   (d) laches and estoppel attributable to owner of prior mark and indicative of lack of confusion.

(11) The extent to which the applicant has a right to exclude others from use of its mark on its goods.

(12) The extent of potential confusion, i.e., whether *de minimis* or substantial.

(13) Any other established fact probative of the effect of use.[111]

DILUTION

A third party may seek to cancel a trademark registration that is less than five years old on the basis that the registration is likely to "dilute" public recognition of a famous mark.[112] Under the Lanham Act, a mark is considered famous for dilution purposes if the mark is widely recognized by consumers within the United States as a designated source identifier for the trademark owner's goods or services. However, showing that a mark has garnered fame for dilution purposes is difficult to establish because many factors must be assessed to determine whether a mark has achieved the status of "famous." To establish a mark has become famous, the third party essentially has to prove the mark has become a household name.[113]

EX PARTE EXPUNGEMENT AND REEXAMINATION PROCEEDINGS

In 2021, the USPTO introduced two new proceedings that could serve as bases for canceling a trademark registration: *ex parte* expungement and reexamination proceedings. *Ex parte* means on behalf of one party without notice to the other party. Expungement and reexamination proceedings are ways to challenge unused registered trademarks that are more efficient and less expensive than commencing a cancellation proceeding. To initiate either of these proceedings, a third party seeking cancellation files either an expungement or reexamination petition with the director of the USPTO. Thereafter, the USPTO handles the proceeding without any further involvement from the third party. Here is the catch: for a petition to be accepted and successful, it must satisfy and comply with strict procedural and evidentiary requirements. If these requirements are not met, the petition will not be accepted. Note that expungement and reexamination proceedings may also be initiated by the director of the USPTO (or a delegate of the director) *sua sponte*, meaning the USPTO can also initiate these proceedings on its own and without prompting from a third party.

Expungement Proceedings

The goal of an expungement proceeding is to cancel all or part of a trademark registration because the mark was never used in commerce in the United States in connection with the goods or services identified in the registration. If the mark was never used in commerce, this means the trademark owner falsely claimed use of the mark to obtain federal registration. As previously discussed, making false claims or misrepresentations to the USPTO during the registration process is grounds for cancellation. This type of proceeding is available for three to ten years after the trademark registration date.[114]

Reexamination Proceedings

The goal of a reexamination proceeding is to cancel all or part of a trademark registration on the basis that the registered mark was not in use in commerce in connection with the registered goods or services in the United States on or before the relevant date. The relevant date for determining whether the mark was in use depends on whether the trademark application was a use-based application or an intent-to-use application. If it was a use-based application, the relevant date is the application filing date. If it was an intent-to-use application, the relevant date is the day the applicant asserted commencement of use.[115] An *ex parte* reexamination must be requested within the first five years after registration of the trademark.

Note that it is possible for a trademark owner to unknowingly misrepresent the use of a mark because they do not fully understand the meaning of the information requested in the trademark application—for example, the meaning or scope of the term "use in commerce."

If you are faced with a situation in which a third party is seeking to cancel your registration or if you as a third party believe that it may be necessary to initiate a trademark cancellation proceeding, I strongly recommend that you engage a trademark attorney to address the situation. Your attorney can help you review the trademark applications or subsequent renewal filings to avoid unintentionally misstating any facts that could potentially cause your trademark rights to be lost.

In the next chapter, I summarize the key points addressed in the previous chapters.

CHAPTER 12

Summary of Key Points

I WANT TO TAKE A MOMENT TO ACKNOWLEDGE YOU FOR YOUR commitment to your business and for making sure its brands are protected. I know you are committed because you have gotten to this point in the book. Of course, this assumes you did not skip all the other chapters just to review the key points. If you did, no judgment on my part; time is a precious commodity. But if this is you, I urge you to take the time to read the prior chapters to understand the significance of brand protection. As I have said before and truly believe, knowledge is power!

You are now more knowledgeable than most business owners on this topic and have a leg up. Congratulations! It is now up to you as a business leader to take the necessary steps to protect your company's brands.

Let's review what you have learned.

INTRODUCTION
In the introduction, you learned how this book would support you in your commitment to the success of your company and the protection of your brands.

CHAPTER 1
In chapter one, you learned about the importance of not delaying your actions because doing so can end up negatively impacting

your ability to protect your brands and obtain federal trademark protection so that you have exclusive rights to use your trademark with the associated goods or services. You also learned about the benefits of brand protection, that IP assets can comprise a large part of a company's value, and that by protecting your IP assets, you can increase the value of your business.

CHAPTER 2

In chapter two, you learned about the ten common mistakes that leave your brand unprotected. In particular, you learned that merely registering your company name with a secretary of state or obtaining an available domain name does not provide you with exclusive rights to use the name. The only thing that accomplishes exclusive rights to a brand in the United States is obtaining a federal trademark registration through the USPTO.

You also learned the importance of being proactive with securing your trademark rights because even though you may be the first to use a trademark, this does not automatically stop a competitor from being able to obtain national trademark rights. You learned about the importance of conducting a comprehensive trademark search. You also learned the importance of conducting routine reviews of your IP assets to make sure that you have the necessary protections in place. You also learned that correctly stating dates of first use in a trademark application and keeping supporting evidence is critical because not doing so can result in your trademark being canceled. You learned that if you are selling your goods or services, or intend to, outside of the United States, you should consider protecting your brand in those other jurisdictions. You also learned the importance of having a budget for IP protection and the benefits of hiring an experienced brand protection attorney sooner versus later to guide you with the trademark process and help implement your brand protection strategies.

CHAPTER 3

In chapter three, you learned, through real-life examples, what can happen if your brand name is similar to another company's brand name, including expensive litigation fees, the possibility of steep monetary damages, and prison time that can apply. You also learned the importance of timely addressing cease and desist letters and why it is best to engage an attorney to assist you with doing so. You also learned that although you may operate your business under the veil of a business entity, it is possible to be held personally liable for trademark infringement, in which case your personal assets could be at risk. Furthermore, you learned that doing things incorrectly can result in the costly and distracting exercise of having to rebrand your company's goods or services. You also learned it is important to speak with your insurance agent to explore the possibility of having IP insurance protection in place in the event you are sued for infringement, as the cost of litigation can be astronomical.

CHAPTER 4

In chapter four, you learned about the four general categories of intellectual property: trademarks, copyrights, patents, and trade secrets. You learned that you must have permission and obtain a license to use someone else's creative work, or risk being sued. You also learned about the benefits of obtaining copyright registrations and the importance of using work-for-hire agreements to ensure your company is the exclusive owner of any and all intellectual property created by employees or contractors.

As for patents, remember that time is of the essence to ensure patent protection. A patent application must be filed within one year of publicly disclosing the invention. The first person to file a patent application will secure priority for the invention, and filing a provisional patent application is a way to have the earliest patent filing date.

As for maintaining trade secrets, you learned the importance of only sharing information on a need-to-know basis.

Additionally, in chapter four, you learned the way to identify what IP assets you have is to work with an IP attorney who will help you by conducting an IP audit and work with you in creating a plan to protect and enforce your IP rights.

CHAPTER 5

In chapter five, we did a deep dive into trademark fundamentals. We reviewed common types of trademarks such as word marks, design marks, and slogans, and we explored nontraditional types of marks such as sound, color, scent, motion, and hologram marks. I also shared various examples of the different types of marks to help you distinguish them and give you a sense of the types of trademarks you currently have and the types of trademarks you may want to create and protect. You also learned how trademark rights are created; the difference between common law rights, state trademark registration, and federal trademark registration; and the difference between the Principal Register and the Supplemental Register. I also explained you can obtain protection of trademarks for digital assets in the metaverse and informed you about the various scam notices you may receive after filing a trademark application.

WHY BRAND PROTECTION MATTERS

CHAPTER 6

In chapter six, I addressed how you can determine whether the brand name you have created is entitled to federal protection and what you should consider when creating brand names to increase your chances of being able to obtain a trademark registration with the USPTO. You learned that generic marks are the weakest type of mark and not entitled to federal protection. You learned that descriptive marks will, at best, be entitled to protection on the Supplemental Register and ineligible for registration on the Principal Register until the trademark owner can show the mark has acquired distinctiveness. You also learned that suggestive marks are marks that imply the quality of the goods or services and may be registered on the Principal Register. The strongest types of marks are arbitrary and fanciful marks: arbitrary marks being actual words that have no association with the goods or services with which they are associated, and fanciful marks being invented or made-up words with no meaning in any language. You should now have a better understanding of the important factors to consider when selecting names to represent your brand.

CHAPTER 7

In chapter seven, you learned how to determine whether you are using a brand name that is similar to another company's and what to do if you find out that is the case. You also learned how to determine whether the brand name you have chosen is available for use in association with the goods or services you intend to sell, and whether your chosen mark would be entitled to federal trademark rights. Importantly, you now know that before you embark on spending thousands of dollars to advertise a certain brand name, it is best to conduct a comprehensive trademark search with the assistance of a trademark attorney to ensure you are not infringing on another entity's trademark rights and putting you and your company at risk of trademark infringement litigation.

CHAPTER 8

In chapter eight, you learned about the USPTO's trademark application process and what information you will need when submitting a trademark application. You also learned you can be proactive and file an intent-to-use trademark application if you want to secure and protect a mark before you begin to use it in commerce and about the benefits of doing so. You are also now familiar with the trademark application timeline and the various steps involved in procuring a federally registered trademark. You also know that filing a trademark application does not automatically create registered trademark rights.

CHAPTER 9

In chapter nine, you learned common reasons why the USPTO refuses or rejects trademark applications and that statistics reveal you can minimize your chances of rejection, and increase your chances of success, by hiring an experienced trademark attorney to work with you on the trademark application process. You also learned that simple, unintended mistakes can completely derail your trademark application and, if not corrected, cause your mark to be abandoned. You also learned about the types of marks that are commonly rejected by examiners, opposition proceedings, and how to appeal an adverse trademark determination, if necessary.

CHAPTER 10

In chapter ten, you learned what you need to do after you have obtained a registered trademark to protect your rights and keep the trademark active. You learned that it is the trademark owner's responsibility to maintain and preserve trademark rights and that these responsibilities do not end once the mark is registered with the USPTO. Rather, you have ongoing obligations to use the mark in association with the goods or services identified in the registration. You also learned about your duty to comply with the USPTO's maintenance filing requirements at various intervals: the first interval being between the fifth and sixth year after the registration date, the next being between the ninth and tenth year after the registration date, and every ten years thereafter (i.e., between the 19th and 20th years, 29th and 30th years, et cetera). You also learned that if someone is not minding the shop, so to speak, the renewal deadlines can be missed, and that if this happens, federal trademark rights will be lost. In addition, you learned that when you submit your first maintenance filing, you may claim incontestable rights to the trademark, which provides certain important benefits to have in the event a trademark dispute arises. Further, you learned the importance of policing your trademark and taking action to stop infringers from using the same or similar mark, or risk losing your federal trademark rights. You learned this may be done through regular trademark watches and by sending out cease and desist letters.

CHAPTER 11

In chapter 11, you learned that even if you obtained a registered trademark, you may still be subject to attack in the form of a trademark cancellation proceeding. You learned about the different types of trademark cancellation proceedings. You learned that the trademark may be deemed abandoned, resulting in a loss of trademark rights, if you stop using the mark in commerce in connection with the goods or services for more than three years, or if there is evidence that the trademark owner does not intend to resume use of the mark. You learned the importance of being accurate in the trademark application, and that errors and mis-statements can come back to haunt you, leaving your registration potentially worthless or canceled if the mark is challenged. You also now know that you should only specify in the application the goods or services that you are selling or intend to sell in associa-tion with the mark. If the identification of goods or services is too broad, or if you are not using the mark in association with all the identified goods or services, you can lose your trademark rights if the mark is challenged. You learned that if a trademark is not policed and it is allowed to be used as a noun or verb, becoming a commonly used or generic term, trademark rights may be lost. Further, you learned the numerous factors the TTAB considers when evaluating a likelihood of confusion claim.

And now, in chapter 12, you are being reminded of the key points and takeaways you have learned, and that will hopefully be of great value to you.

CHAPTER 13

Empowered to Lead, Grow Your Business, and Take Action to Protect Your Brand

I AM PERSONALLY THRILLED YOU HAVE TAKEN THE TIME TO READ this book, and I want you to know that I do not take that lightly. I know that as entrepreneurs and business owners, there are many different things that need our attention, and we often wish there were more hours in a day. Knowledge is power! I trust that you now have clarity around the subject of brand protection and are empowered to have a productive and efficient conversation with a brand protection attorney. Once you do so, you will have peace of mind knowing your brand assets will be properly protected and that you will not be leaving the protection to chance, crossing your fingers and hoping it was done correctly.

I am incredibly passionate about helping businesses thrive and empowering business owners to avoid costly mistakes. I am excited for what you now know and all the good you will accomplish in the world. You see, if you are reading this book, I know you are committed to doing things correctly. As the leader of your business, you are now empowered to take action so that your business grows on a solid foundation. Congratulations!

Thank you for reading this book and trusting me in the process. I truly hope you have found it to be a worthwhile investment of your time and that you have been enlightened through the process. I feel inspired to share a story with you about how I learned about investing and the benefit of doing so.

When I was about five years old and living in South Africa, my father would give me an allowance in the form of coins, which I would use to buy chocolate and sweets at the local convenience store, referred to as a café (pronounced kah-fee). One day, my father explained that if I did not spend the money and let him hold it, not only would he give me my allowance the following week but he would also give me additional money as interest on the money I did not spend. I thought this was the best thing I had ever heard at the time and was delighted that by not spending the money, I would have more money. Likewise, I hope you feel that by not using the time spent reading this book to do other things, your investment of time in reading this book has paid off or will pay off for you in the future.

In my experience, there are two types of buyers of legal services: those who want the least expensive solution and those who value making sure it is done correctly because they understand the cost of not doing so is too great. For those of you who prefer the least expensive solution (no judgment here), I want you to know that, in my practice, I have been retained to fix trademark applications that were done through do-it-yourself processes and nonlawyers. Many clients have come to me to help clean up the messes that were created by not doing it correctly in the first place. Oftentimes, this ends up costing the trademark owner more money than it would have cost to do it correctly from the beginning.

For those of you who value making sure you have correctly protected your trademark assets and are willing to pay for that service from an experienced brand protection attorney, I am here for you. I am here for those of you who have the most on the line to get it done right. If you are someone who has invested your entire life's savings in your business concept, who wants to keep your assets and not subject them to unnecessary risk, and who knows there is a long-term benefit to doing brand protection correctly the first time, I am here for you. If you want a strategic thinker who will hold your hand and help you think through the process, then we may be a good fit for each other. Regardless of whether you work with my firm or not, I urge you to not take the cheap way out, as the cost and potential negative impacts of doing so can be too great.

I would love to hear your feedback on the value reading this book provided you, any "aha moments," and what additional intellectual property information you would find valuable to learn about. Please feel free to email (see the Additional Information section at the back of this book for my contact information).

I invite you to stay in touch with me, connect with me on social media, subscribe to my firm's YouTube channel, sign up for my firm's newsletter, and check out Brand Protection University® at www.BrandProtection.Law (see the Additional Information section for links to my social media channels and to sign up for my firm's newsletter). Finally, my friends, if you feel inspired to do so, please do not delay and contact my law firm to schedule a consultation.

I am cheering for your success!

Acknowledgments

As the saying goes, "It takes a village," and I am immensely grateful for my village. I have the most amazing, supportive family and friends in my life who have encouraged me to write this book, cheered me on along the way, and allowed me to pick their brain at all hours of the day and night. To each and every one of you—a heartfelt, huge thank you! You are greatly appreciated!

To my precious son, Jake, you are my inspiration. Thank you for your love, support, and understanding while I focused on writing this book. Your encouraging words and amazing hugs while I typed away meant the world to me.

To my love, Jon, your unconditional love and encouragement have been my rock. I am the luckiest woman in the world to have you by my side, cheering me on, and being so incredibly understanding of the time commitment required to birth this book.

To my lifelong bestie Evan, thank you from the bottom of my heart for always being one of my biggest cheerleaders of all time.

To my brother Mark, Uncle Gary, Auntie Shirley, Uncle Ellis, and to my special friends Alan, Carol, Jackie, Joan, Maryanna, and Tanija, your unwavering support has sustained me throughout this journey. Thank you for believing in me and loving me.

To my dear friend and colleague, Philip Wiese, thank you for being my beta reader, and for your invaluable feedback, candor, and encouraging late-night chats. Your friendship and knowing you have my back mean the world to me.

To Ashley Mansour, my dynamic writing coach, this book would not have been possible without the structure of your writing and publishing programs along with your invaluable guidance, unwavering support, and your amazing team of professionals. Your wisdom, belief in my work, and encouragement have been instrumental in bringing this book to fruition.

To Jessica Reino, I thoroughly enjoyed working with you. Your keen editorial eye, constructive feedback, and thought-provoking questions elevated my manuscript to new heights. Thank you for your insightful contributions and enthusiasm about the topic.

To Chelsea Morning, thank you for managing the publishing process with grace and for keeping me on track. Your attention to all the details made a difference.

Further, to those special people with very busy lives who went above and beyond to take the time to read my manuscript and provide an endorsement, I am deeply grateful.

Finally, to you, my readers, thank you for taking the time to read this book. My thoughts of you and your commitment to your business's success fueled my determination to complete this project.

Photography by Ginny Dixon

LEE-ANNE "L.A." PERKINS IS A TOP-RATED BRAND PROTECTION attorney (a.k.a. an intellectual property attorney and a trademark attorney) in the State of Florida, where she has been a member of the Florida Bar since 1996 and has served as the president of the South Palm Beach County Bar Association. She is the founder and CEO of L.A. Perkins Law Firm PLLC, doing business as Perkins Law—Brand Protection, which she founded in 2013 following her experience as a partner in two highly regarded large law firms. She has represented an array of clients, from individuals to Fortune 100 companies in various industries, and has successfully litigated intellectual property cases in federal and state courts, including jury trials.

L.A. focuses her practice on helping innovative, visionary business owners, executives, and entrepreneurs identify and protect their intellectual property assets, maintain their IP assets, and enforce their rights when necessary. She is passionate about guiding her clients in the selection of their brands and securing their brand assets so they can build their businesses on a solid foundation with peace of mind positioned for success.

She has been recognized by clients, colleagues, opposing counsel, judges, and various attorney rating services for the quality of her work and professionalism. For more than 15 years, she has held the highest rating from Martindale-Hubbell Law Directory—now referred to as AV Preeminent®—which indicates the highest level of skill, integrity, and professional conduct. This distinction is awarded to approximately 10 percent of all United States attorneys. She has also received the prestigious Florida Super Lawyers® designation for intellectual property litigation, a recognition achieved by no more than 5 percent of attorneys in each state. She was also recognized as a top lawyer in intellectual property by *The Boca Raton Observer* and *Palm Beach Illustrated* and is a Florida Supreme Court-certified mediator. She is committed to making a difference. For more information on L.A.'s background, go to *www.BrandProtection.Law/la-perkins/*.

Additional Information

To download the resources referenced in the book, visit *www.BrandProtection.Law/Resources*

For more information on brand protection, go to Brand Protection University™ at *www.BrandProtection.Law/brand-protection-university*

To learn more about the author, visit *www.BrandProtection.Law/la-perkins*

To contact the author regarding speaking engagements, email: *WBPM@BrandProtection.Law*

For all media inquiries or other questions, email: *Media@BrandProtection.Law*

To sign up for the Perkins Law—Brand Protection newsletter, go to *www.BrandProtection.Law/subscribe-to-our-newsletter*

To conduct a trademark search of the USPTO database, go to *tmsearch.uspto.gov/search/search-information*

To access the USPTO Design Search Code Manual, go to *tmdesigncodes.uspto.gov*

To connect with the author on social media, go to
LinkedIn (personal): *linkedin.com/
in/l-a-perkins-brand-protection-attorney-3548768*

LinkedIn (company): *linkedin.com/company/78335247*

YouTube: *youtube.com/channel/UCCTn1X8reHO1zIUHfJP6sIg*

Facebook: *facebook.com/PerkinsLawBrandProtection*

Instagram: *instagram.com/brandprotection.law*

Author contact information:
    L.A. Perkins, Esq.
    Perkins Law – Brand Protection
    2295 NW Corporate Boulevard, Suite 117,
    Boca Raton, Florida 33431
    Telephone: (561) 467-4001
    Email: *WBPM@BrandProtection.Law*

SAMPLE SCAM LETTER

PATENT & TRADEMARK OFFICE
Protecting Intellectual Property in the United States

Form: Section 8

Case Id: 2023A12PR_41880

PENDING TRADEMARK CANCELLATION

Your Trademark is about to expire. Renewal date: Dec.22.2023

1. Correspondence address:

    L.A. PERKINS LAW FIRM PLLC
    5301 N FEDERAL HWY STE 110
    BOCA RATON FL 33487-4914

2. Graphic representation:

TRADEMARK GENIE

TRADEMARK RENEWAL OFFER UNDER DECLARATION SECTION 8

3. Trademark Name:	6. Registration Number:
TRADEMARK GENIE	6228449
4. Type:	**7. Number of Classes:**
Service Mark	1
5. Registration Date:	**8. Classes:**
Dec.22.2020	045

A

9. IMPORTANT INFORMATION - PLEASE READ

In order to renew your trademark, please sign and return this document in the enclose prepaid envelope. Once your signed form and payment has been received and processed by us, the renewal process will start. **The trademark stated on this document will be renewed for another period of five (5) years. The renewal fee for the 5-year period is $ 1090 including one class. Each subsequent class is debited with a fee of $ 520. Note: if not renewed in time, your exclusive rights to that mark may be terminated.** By signing this document, you place an order for filling the renewal of the identified trademark registration for the classes identified in this form and confirm that you comply with the Terms and Conditions of the order form. By returning and signing this document, you also empower Patent & Trademark Office to conduct and perform the renewal process on your behalf. You will receive a confirmation from us once the trademark renewal is completed. This is an optional offer. This document is not a bill. Patent & Trademark Office is a private company, not associated with any official governmental organizations. Patent & Trademark Office provides the expertise that modern businesses need to navigate the Patent and Trademark Office's registration and renewal process. If you have any questions regarding the renewal of your trademark, please contact Patent & Trademark Office renewal department via e-mail: **info@pto-us.com** or telephone: **(800) 983-4701**

10. Declaration of Incontestability:

☐ Please check box if you are interested in filling a Trademark Incontestability (15 U.S.C. § 1065) for an extra Fee $ 400 per class

11. Section 8 Filling Fees:

		12. SIGN AND RETURN IN THE ENCLOSED ENVELOPE:
One class renewal fee:	$ 1090	
Subsequent class(es):	$ 0	Name and title (Enter appropriate title or nature of relationship to the owner/holder).
TOTAL:	$ 1090	(e-mail) required
		(Date and Signature) required

Patent & Trademark Office, correspondence address: 19125 North Creek Parkway, Suite 120, Bothell, WA 98011
tel.: 1(800) 983-4701 Business hours: Mon-Fri from 9:00 am to 3:00 pm EDT
www.pto-us.com

167

Endnotes

1   Deborah R. Gerhardt and Jon P. McClanahan, *Do Trademark Lawyers Matter?*, 16 STAN. TECH. L. REV., 583 (2013).

2   Jeff Bater, "14,000 take oath of citizenship," upi.com, Jul. 4, 1986. https://www.upi.com/Archives/1986/07/04/14000-take-oath-of-citizenship/1216520833600/.

3   15 U.S.C. § 1117 (c)(1) and (2).

4   Steven Miller, "Do You Have the Time? Mickey Mouse Watches at Disney Parks," disneyparks.disney.go.com, Nov. 29, 2010. https://disneyparks.disney.go.com/blog/2010/11/do-you-have-the-time-mickey-mouse-watches-at-disney-parks/#:~:text=Disney%20watches%20have%20quite%20a,an%20exclusive%20license%20from%20Disney.

5   Ocean Tomo, a part of J.S. Held, Intangible Asset Market Value Study, 2020; https://oceantomo.com/intangible-asset-market-value-study/.

6   Emma Baldwin, "An ounce of prevention is Zorth a pound of cure," Poem Analysis, Oct. 31, 2023. https://poemanalysis.com/proverb/an-ounce-of-prevention-is-worth-a-pound-of-cure/.

7   18 U.S.C. § 2320.

8   18 U.S.C. § 2320 (b).

9   18 U.S.C. § 2320 (b)(1)(A).

10   18 U.S.C. § 2320 (b)(1)(B) and (b)(2)(A) and (b)(3)(A).

11   18 U.S.C. § 2320 (b)(3)(B).

12   18 U.S.C. § 2320 (b)(2)(B).

13   8 U.S.C. § 101(a)(43).

14   *Starbucks Corporation v. Lundberg*, Civil No. 02-948-HA, 9 (D. Or. Nov. 29, 2005).

15   *Id.*

16   *See Lundberg,* Civil No. 02-948-HA, at 15.

17   *Id.* at 12. "Eighty-five percent of consumers who encountered the 'Sambuck's Coffeehouse' name immediately thought of 'Starbucks.'"

18   *Id.* at 21.

19   *Id.*

20   *Id.* at 30.

21   Seattle Times Staff, "Judge Sides with Starbucks in name dispute with Sambuck's," seattletimes.com, Dec. 1, 2005. https://www.seattletimes.com/business/judge-sides-with-starbucks-in-name-dispute-with-sambucks.

22   CNET, "Wrestling Loses WWF to Wildlife," cnet.com, Aug. 2, 2002. https://www.cnet.com/tech/services-and-software/wrestling-loses-wwf-to-wildlife/.

23   *See* [2002] EWCA Civ 196, 21. https://www.casemine.com/judgement/uk/5b46f1fb2c94e0775e7ef55d.

24   *Id.* at 27.

25   *Id.* at 71.

26   140 S. Ct. 1492 (2020).

27   American Intellectual Property Law Association Law Practice Management Committee, REPORT OF THE ECONOMIC SURVEY I-190–I-197 (October 2023).

28   United States Copyright Office, *Copyright Basics*, Sept. 2021, page 4. https://www.copyright.gov/circs/circ01.pdf.

29   *Id.*

30   *Id.*

31   *Id.*

32   *Id.*

33   *Id.*

34 *See* 17 U.S.C. § 504(c)(1).

35 *See* 17 U.S.C. § 504(c)(2).

36 *Stephen Thaler v. Shira Perlmutter, Register of Copyrights and Director of the United States Copyright Office, et al.*, Civil Action No. 22-1564 (BAH), United States District Court for the District of Columbia, Memorandum Opinion, August 18, 2023.

37 *Id.* at 1.

38 *Id.* at 1-2, 15.

39 Leahy-Smith American Invents Act (AIA), 35 U.S.C. §102 and §103 as amended March 16, 2013.

40 Sheldon Brown, "Patent Statistics," Patent Experts, Mar. 22, 2023, https://patentexperts.org/patent/statistics/#:~:text=From%20 2011%2D2020%20the%20USPTO,Design%20Patents%3A%2069.2%25.

41 *Apple, Inc. v. Samsung Electronics Co.*, Case No. 11-CV-01846-LHK, Order Requiring New Trial on Design Patent Damages, *3-4 (N.D. Cal. Oct. 22, 2017) (citing *See Samsung Electronics Co., LTD. v. Apple Inc.*, 137 S. Ct. 429, 434 (2016)).

42 *See Samsung Electronics Co., LTD. v. Apple Inc.*, 137 S. Ct. 429, 433 (2016).

43 *Apple, Inc. v. Samsung Electronics Co., Ltd., et al*, Case No. 11-CV-01846-LHK, Order Requiring New Trial on Design Patent Damages, *1 (N.D. Cal. Oct. 22, 2017).

44 *Apple, Inc. v. Samsung Electronics Co., Ltd., et al*, Case No. 11-CV-01846-LHK, Joint Notice of Settlement and Stipulation of Dismissal with Prejudice, p. 2 (N.D. Cal. June 27, 2018).

45 United States Patent and Trademark Office, "General Information About 35 U.S.C. 161 Plant Patents," uspto.gov, accessed Feb. 13, 2024. https://www.uspto.gov/patents/basics/apply/plant-patent.

46 United States Patent and Trademark Office, "2701 Patent Term [R-07.222]," uspto.gov, accessed Feb. 13, 2024. https://www.uspto.gov/web/offices/pac/mpep/s2701.html#:~:text=This%20patent%20term%20 provision%20is,the%20Hague%20Agreement%20Concerning%20the.

47 *Id.*

48   18 U.S.C. § 1839(3).

49   The Coca-Cola Company, coca-cola.com, accessed Feb. 13, 2024. https://www.coca-cola.com/us/en/brands/coca-cola/products/original#accordion-c55f229edc-item-93131ee8b3.

50   21 C.F.R. 101.4.

51   21 C.F.R. 101.100.

52   21 C.F.R. 101.22.

53   World of Coca-Cola, "Vault of the Secret Formula," worldofcoca-cola.com, accessed Feb. 13, 2024. https://www.worldofcoca-cola.com/explore-inside/explore-vault-secret-formula.

54   World Intellectual Property Organization, "Summary of the Paris Convention for the Protection of Industrial Property (1883)," wipo.com, accessed Feb. 13, 2024. www.wipo.int/treaties/en/ip/paris/summary_paris.html.

55   United States Patent and Trademark Office, "Trademark Status & Document Retrieval (TSDR)," uspto.gov, accessed Feb. 13, 2024. https://tsdr.uspto.gov/#caseNumber=78559133&caseSearchType=US_APPLICATION&caseType=DEFAULT&searchType=statusSearch.

56   United States Patent and Trademark Office, "Trademark Status & Document Retrieval (TSDR)," uspto.gov, accessed Feb. 13, 2024. https://tsdr.uspto.gov/#caseNumber=85222261&caseSearchType=US_APPLICATION&caseType=DEFAULT&searchType=statusSearch.

57   United States Patent and Trademark Office, "Trademark Status & Document Retrieval (TSDR)," uspto.gov, accessed Feb. 13, 2024. https://tsdr.uspto.gov/#caseNumber=87915979&caseSearchType=US_APPLICATION&caseType=DEFAULT&searchType=statusSearch.

58   United States Patent and Trademark Office, "Trademark Status & Document Retrieval (TSDR)," uspto.gov, accessed Feb. 13, 2024. https://tsdr.uspto.gov/#caseNumber=87915979&caseSearchType=US_APPLICATION&caseType=DEFAULT&searchType=statusSearch.

59   United States Patent and Trademark Office, "Trademark Status & Document Retrieval (TSDR)," uspto.gov, accessed Feb. 13, 2024.

https://tsdr.uspto.gov/#caseNumber=86983875&caseSearchType=US_
APPLICATION&caseType=DEFAULT&searchType=statusSearch.

60   United States Patent and Trademark Office, "Trademark Status &
     Document Retrieval (TSDR)," uspto.gov, accessed Feb. 13, 2024. https://
     tsdr.uspto.gov/#caseNumber=73162799&caseSearchType=US_APPLI-
     CATION&caseType=DEFAULT&searchType=statusSearch.

61   United States Patent and Trademark Office, "Trademark Status &
     Document Retrieval (TSDR)," uspto.gov, accessed Feb. 13, 2024. https://
     tsdr.uspto.gov/#caseNumber=71254695&caseSearchType=US_APPLI-
     CATION&caseType=DEFAULT&searchType=statusSearch.

62   United States Patent and Trademark Office, "Trademark Status &
     Document Retrieval (TSDR)," uspto.gov, accessed Feb. 13, 2024. https://
     tsdr.uspto.gov/#caseNumber=73823843&caseSearchType=US_APPLI-
     CATION&caseType=DEFAULT&searchType=statusSearch.

63   United States Patent and Trademark Office, "Trademark Status &
     Document Retrieval (TSDR)," uspto.gov, accessed Feb. 13, 2024. https://
     tsdr.uspto.gov/#caseNumber=73304275&caseSearchType=US_APPLI-
     CATION&caseType=DEFAULT&searchType=statusSearch.

64   United States Patent and Trademark Office, "Trademark Status &
     Document Retrieval (TSDR)," uspto.gov, accessed Feb. 13, 2024. https://
     tsdr.uspto.gov/#caseNumber=78567713&caseSearchType=US_APPLI-
     CATION&caseType=DEFAULT&searchType=statusSearch.

65   United States Patent and Trademark Office, "Trademark Status &
     Document Retrieval (TSDR)," uspto.gov, accessed Feb. 13, 2024. https://
     tsdr.uspto.gov/#caseNumber=98038944&caseSearchType=US_APPLI-
     CATION&caseType=DEFAULT&searchType=statusSearch.

66   United States Patent and Trademark Office, "Trademark Status &
     Document Retrieval (TSDR)," uspto.gov, accessed Feb. 13, 2024. https://
     tsdr.uspto.gov/#caseNumber=97806875&caseSearchType=US_APPLI-
     CATION&caseType=DEFAULT&searchType=statusSearch.

67   United States Patent and Trademark Office, "Trademark Status &
     Document Retrieval (TSDR)," uspto.gov, accessed Feb. 13, 2024. https://
     tsdr.uspto.gov/#caseNumber=88170627&caseSearchType=US_APPLI-
     CATION&caseType=DEFAULT&searchType=statusSearch.

68   United States Patent and Trademark Office, "Trademark Status & Document Retrieval (TSDR)," uspto.gov, accessed Feb. 13, 2024. https://tsdr.uspto.gov/#caseNumber=77726532&caseSearchType=US_APPLICATION&caseType=DEFAULT&searchType=statusSearch.

69   United States Patent and Trademark Office, "Trademark Status & Document Retrieval (TSDR)," uspto.gov, accessed Feb. 13, 2024. https://tsdr.uspto.gov/#caseNumber=75883661&caseSearchType=US_APPLICATION&caseType=DEFAULT&searchType=statusSearch.

70   *In re Upper Deck Co.*, 59 USPQ2d 1688, 1693 (TTAB 2001).

71   *See* 15 U.S.C. § 1052(a).

72   United States Patent and Trademark Office, "Caution: Scam alert," uspto.gov, accessed Feb. 13, 2024. https://www.uspto.gov/trademarks/protect/caution-misleading-notices.

73   *United States v. Suhorukovs*, 6:20-cr-00210, U.S. District Court for the District of South Carolina (2021).

74   TMEP, 1209.01 (b), Merely Descriptive Marks.

75   United States Patent and Trademark Office, "Goods and services," uspto.gov, accessed Feb. 13, 2024. https://www.uspto.gov/trademarks/basics/goods-and-services.

76   *Id.*

77   United States Patent and Trademark Office, "Nice Agreement current edition version-general remarks, class headings and explanatory notes," uspto.gov, accessed Feb. 13, 2024. https://www.uspto.gov/trademarks/trademark-updates-and-announcements/nice-agreement-current-edition-version-general-remarks#class-headings-with-explanatory-notes; https://idm-tmng.uspto.gov/id-master-list-public.html.

78   "Fiscal Year Application Filings (classes)" graph, USPTO, *Trademarks Data Q1 2023 At A Glance,* (2023), https://www.uspto.gov/dashboard/trademarks/.

79   "New Registrations by Fiscal Year (classes)" graph, USPTO, *Trademarks Data Q1 2023 At A Glance,* (2023), https://www.uspto.gov/dashboard/trademarks/.

80   https://www.uspto.gov/learning-and-resources/support-centers/pub-
      lic-search-facility/using-public-search-facility (see USPTO, Historical
      collections, Trademark-related historical collections, The Trademark
      Bound Volumes Register); https://news.wttw.com/2022/03/21/
      fascinating-stories-behind-world-s-oldest-logos.

81   Peter Smith, *Underwood's Deviled Ham: The Oldest Trademark Still in
      Use*, SMITHSONIAN MUSEUM (Mar. 9, 2012), https://www.smithso-
      nianmag.com/arts-culture/underwoods-deviled-ham-the-oldest-trade-
      mark-still-in-use-119136583/#:~:text=On%20November%2029%2C%20
      1870%2C%20the,brand%2Dnew%20U.S.%20Patent%20Office.

82   *Id.*

83   Merriam-Webster, "entremets," merram-webster.com, accessed Feb. 13,
      2024. https://www.merriam-webster.com/dictionary/entremets.

84   Merriam-Webster, "repast," merram-webster.com, accessed Feb. 13,
      2024. https://www.merriam-webster.com/dictionary/repasts.

85   Deborah R. Gerhardt and Jon P. McClanahan, *Do Trademark Lawyers
      Matter?*, 16 STAN. TECH. L. REV., 583, 619 (2013).

86   Deborah R. Gerhardt and Jon J. Lee, *A Tale of Four Decades: Lessons
      from USPTO Trademark Prosecution Data*, THE TRADEMARK
      REPORTER, 112, 6 (2022) at 895-902.

87   Deborah R. Gerhardt and Jon J. Lee, *A Tale of Four Decades: Lessons
      from USPTO Trademark Prosecution Data*, THE TRADEMARK
      REPORTER, 112, 6 (2022) at 897.

88   Deborah Gerhardt and Jon McClanahan, *Do Trademark Lawyers
      Matter?*, 16 Stan. Tech. L. Rev 583, 618 (2013), http://stlr.stanford.edu/
      pdf/dotrademarklawyersmatter.pdf.

89   Deborah R. Gerhardt and Jon J. Lee, *A Tale of Four Decades: Lessons
      from USPTO Trademark Prosecution Data*, THE TRADEMARK
      REPORTER, 112, 6 (2022) at 897.

90   United States Patent and Trademark Office, "Possible Grounds for
      Refusal of a Mark," uspto.gov, accessed Feb. 13, 2024. https://www.
      uspto.gov/trademarks/additional-guidance-and-resources/possi-
      ble-grounds-refusal-mark#:~:text=The%20USPTO%20may%20be%20
      required,a%20trademark%20application%20is%20filed.

91   TMEP § 1209.01(b).

92   *In re Johanna Farms Inc.*, 8 U.S.P.Q.2d 1408, 1988 WL 252411, at *5-6 n. 7 (T.T.A.B. 1988).

93   TMEP § 1211.01.

94   *Id.*

95   *In re Rebo High Definition Studio, Inc.*, 15 U.S.P.Q.2d 1314, 1990 WL 354507, at *1 (T.T.A.B. 1990).

96   *In re JT Tobacconists*, 59 U.S.P.Q.2d 1080, 2001 WL 630647 (T.T.A.B. 2001).

97   *In re Compania de Licores Internaciionales S.A.*, 102 U.S.P.Q.2d 1841, 2012 WL 1267898 (T.T.A.B. 2012).

98   37 C.F.R. §2.161(6)(ii).

99   37 C.F.R. §2.161(6)(ii).

100 *See* 37 C.F.R. §§ 2.161(b), 7.37(b).

101 18 U.S.C. § 2320(b)(1)(A).

102 37 C.F.R. § 11.14(e).

103 37 C.F.R. § 2.2.

104 TMEP § 1209.01(c)(i).

105 Bentley University, "Popular Brands Had Their Trademarks Revoked," Bentley.edu, Mar. 10, 2018. https://www.bentley.edu/news/popular-brands-had-their-trademarks-revoked-law#:~:text=Escalator%20was%20owned%20by%20Otis,in%20a%20court%20of%20law.

106 *Bayer Co. v. United Drug Co.*, 272 F. 505 (S.D.N.Y. 1921).

107 Robert B.G. Horowitz, "Attention Rights Holders: The Lessons On Genericism From Thermos Remain Critical," WORLD TRADEMARK REVIEW, Feb. 28, 2014, at 78-79, file:///C:/Users/Owner/OneDrive%20-%20L.A.%20Perkins%20Law%20Firm%20PLLC/Downloads/pattention-rights-holders-the-lessons-on-genericism-from-thermos-remain-criticalp%20(2).pdf.

108   *Elliot v. Google Inc.*, 860 F. 3d 1151 (2017).

109   15 U.S.C. § 1052(d).

110   476 F.2d 1357, 1361 (C.C.P.A. 1973).

111   *Id.*

112   15 U.S.C. § 1125(c).

113   *Coach Servs., Inc. v. Triumph Learning LLC*, 668 F.3d 1356, 1373 (Fed. Cir. 2012).

114   United States Patent and Trademark Office, "USPTO implements the Trademark Modernization Act," uspto.gov, accessed Feb. 13, 2024. https://www.uspto.gov/trademarks/laws/2020-modernization-act?utm_campaign=subscriptioncenter&utm_content=&utm_medium=e-mail&utm_name=&utm_source=govdelivery&utm_term=#proceed-ings.

115   15 U.S.C. § 1066b(b); 37 C.F.R. § 2.91(a)(2).

www.ingramcontent.com/pod-product-compliance
Lightning Source LLC
Chambersburg PA
CBHW071214210326
41597CB00016B/1810